TODAY'S WRITERS
AND THEIR WORKS

HA
JIN

Marc Schumann

Cavendish
Square

New York

Library of Congress Cataloging-in-Publication Data

Schumann, Marc. • Ha Jin / Marc Schumann. • p. cm.—(Today's writers and their works)
Includes bibliographical references and index. • Summary: "Explores the life,
work, and themes of author Ha Jin"—Provided by publisher.
ISBN 978-1-62712-152-1 (hardcover) ISBN 978-1-62712-146-0 (paperback)
ISBN 978-1-60870-760-7 (ebook)
1. Jin, Ha, 1956—Juvenile literature. 2. Authors, American—20th century—Biography—Juvenile literature. 3. Chinese American authors—Biography—Juvenile literature. I. Title.
PS3560.I6Z87 2011 • 813'.54—dc22 • [B] • 2010048841

Art Director: Anahid Hamparian

Series Designer: Alicia Mikles • Photo research by Lindsay Aveilhe

The photographs in this book are used by permission and through the courtesy of:
Cover photo by Robert S. Abrahamson/Time & Life Pictures/Getty Images; Mike Segar/Reuters: p. 4; Frank Fischbeck/Time & Life Pictures/Getty Images: p. 8; Keystone/Getty Images: p. 11; Rolls Press/Popperfoto/Getty Images: p. 13; Xinhua/AP Photo: p. 17; The Art Archive/Bibliothèque des Arts Décoratifs Paris/Gianni Dagli Orti: p. 20; AP Photo: p. 23; Courtesy of Brandeis University: p. 26; Images.com/Corbis: p. 28; Dario Mitidieri/Getty Images: p. 30; Courtesy of © 1990 Phoenix Poets, University of Chicago Press: p. 33; Courtesy of © 1998 Vintage International, Random House, Inc.: p. 37; J. Cuinieres/Roger Viollet/Getty Images: p. 42; G P Bowater/Alamy: p. 46; Diane Bondareff/AP Photo: p. 50; Marie Mathelin/ Roger-Viollet/The Image Works: p. 52; The Granger Collection, NYC: p. 53; Zhou Thong/Akg Images: p. 56; North Wind Picture Archives via AP Images: p. 59; Courtesy of © 2005 Vintage, NYC, Random House, Inc.: p. 79; Time Life Pictures/USIA/National Archives/Getty Images: p. 81; AP Photo: p. 90; Imaginechina via AP Images: p. 97.

CONTENTS

Ha Jin (*left*), who won the National Book Award for *Waiting* in 1999, stands with fellow award winners, and gold medal winner Oprah Winfrey (*center*), at the gala honoring them.

INTRODUCTION

CHINESE-AMERICAN AUTHOR HA JIN has achieved international success with the reading public, and acclaim from critics. His stories and novels have vividly chronicled the most significant events in late twentieth-century Chinese life, while more recently exploring the American immigrant experience and international traumas such as war and political persecution. Since leaving China permanently after the Tiananmen Square massacre of 1989, a national tragedy in which the Chinese army slaughtered hundreds of student demonstrators in Beijing, Ha Jin has embraced his role as an outsider. His books have frequently challenged the repressive Chinese government, and as a result are largely banned there. Still, the universal quality of Ha Jin's writing has prevailed. As his reputation has soared, Ha Jin has chosen the United States as his home and, increasingly, his subject matter.

In many ways, Ha Jin's stunning literary rise in the 1990s was unlikely. Growing up, he was barely literate, and the thought of writing books would have seemed to him a bizarre notion. He dreamed of becoming a military officer like his father and bringing glory to the country he loved. It was only after six years in the Chinese People's Liberation Army that he began to seek an education. Even after unexpectedly discovering a love of reading in college his plan was to be a professor or critic. It was not until the tragedy at Tiananmen Square that Ha Jin began to see a future for himself as a fiction writer.

After learning of the terrible bloodshed, Ha Jin was outraged. As a patriotic teenager serving in the army, he had desired to defend the Chinese people. Now he watched helplessly as the government declared its own citizens the enemy. The poems and stories that Ha Jin began to write in the coming months and years used his anger as their starting point, exploring the struggle of characters trying to survive under authoritarian power.

In the preface to *Between Silences*, his first book of poems—published in 1990—Ha Jin stated his ambition to "speak for those unfortunate people who suffered, endured, or perished at the bottom of life and who created the history." Although he would later question his own status as spokesman for the Chinese people, this moral purpose inspired much of his early work.

Ha Jin achieved his first major success seven years after Tiananmen, with his first collection of short stories, *Ocean of Words*. The book drew heavily on his experiences in the Chinese army and won praise for what would become Ha Jin's signature blend of hard-edged realism, lively action, and brilliantly satiric humor. Two years later, Ha Jin achieved his breakthrough with the novel *Waiting*, which won America's prestigious National Book Award in 1999, and catapulted its author to international fame. Since *Waiting*, Ha Jin has been prolific, publishing eight books, including his first collection of essays, *The Writer as Migrant*, in 2008.

The excesses of the Cultural Revolution of the 1960s and 1970s were carried out in large part by children, who had been indoctrinated since birth to believe that any act of violence was justified as a means to the Communist ends sought by their leader, Chairman Mao.

1

LIFE AND TIMES

IN THE SPRING OF 1989, Ha Jin's future seemed comfortably set in place. Nearly finished with his doctoral degree in literature at Brandeis University, he would soon return with his wife to China, where they would raise their son and where Ha Jin had accepted an offer to teach at Shandong University. That June, however, the violence at Tiananmen Square shattered his feeling of security. Watching TV in his small campus apartment in Boston, Ha Jin was deeply troubled. For the young scholar, who had given much of his early life to defending his country, the actions of the Chinese government were a painful betrayal. "I was glued to the TV for three days," Ha Jin recalled. "I was in shock. I had served in the army to protect the people. Suddenly the whole thing was reversed. I just couldn't reconcile it [with my own views of China]."

After months of soul-searching, Ha Jin realized he could not live honestly under such a government. America would be his new home, and writing about the lives of his former countrymen his vocation. Although it would be another seven years until Ha Jin broke through with his first collection of stories, his commitment to writing was sealed during the horror of Tiananmen Square. It is from this point that one of the most remarkable careers in contemporary world literature begins.

Early Years

Jin Xuefei, who writes under the pen name Ha Jin, was born February 21, 1956, in the city of Jinzhou, in the northeastern part of China, formerly known as Manchuria. His father was a low-ranking military officer and the family never settled in one place for long. This rootless upbringing made it difficult to build lasting friendships, although Ha Jin has recalled happy memories of playing outside well into the evenings with his four brothers.

Despite his father's privileged position in what many Chinese considered the most glorious and modernized branch of the government—the People's Liberation Army —the Jin family had little money. This only brought them closer together, however, with each of Ha Jin's brothers helping around the house while their father was away. As long as his family stayed together, Ha Jin didn't mind the frequent moving. He remembers the warm affection they shared. But soon, his family would be pulled apart.

Revolution

At the age of only seven, Ha Jin was sent away to boarding school. While he was gone, the Cultural Revolution started. Beginning in 1966, the Cultural Revolution was a bloody ten-year campaign initiated by Communist Party chairman

People like this Chinese landowner, considered an enemy of the state, were often executed in broad daylight during the Cultural Revolution.

Mao Zedong to overturn traditional Chinese society. Mao had taken power in 1949 amid much hope that China would become a fairer and more peaceful country. The Communists vowed to end all class distinctions while empowering the poor, women, and peasants. By 1966, however, Mao's utopian vision had failed. Faced with growing criticism from the Chinese people and the Communist leaders who had largely succeeded him, he designed the Cultural Revolution to reassert Communist values.

Mao's actions brought about the closing of all the country's schools, as entire groups were targeted for "re-education" in the ways of Communist ideology. Intellectuals, artists, and people who came from landowning families were sent to the countryside to perform hard labor. Those who dissented were brutally punished. Mao used volunteer militias such as the Red Guard to implement his vision.

Composed mostly of young people, the Red Guard was absolutely loyal to Mao and shocking in its casual use of violence, often dragging suspected "dissidents" out of their homes and butchering them in broad daylight. In this regard, the members of the Red Guard adhered to Mao's famous statement, "All political power grows out of the barrel of a gun." In all, more than three million Chinese people were killed during this traumatic ten-year period.

Ha Jin was nine years old and in his second year of study when his own school was abruptly closed. When he returned home he found his family in turmoil. All of his father's books were removed from the house and burned in a huge bonfire on the city streets. For the young Ha Jin, the blaze seemed miles high and as long as a city block.

Soon his mother was targeted by the Red Guard because her father was a former landlord who had owned several acres of land before the Communist revolution. "My mother was criticized very severely," Ha Jin recalled. "People did terrible things to her. She was once thrown into a trash can." She was sent away to pick apples in the countryside, a punishment that she endured off and on for several years.

Ha Jin was too young to understand the meaning of the revolution, but the family banded together far more closely in his mother's absence. Ha Jin remembered that neither his father nor his mother complained about Mao's program, or the actions of the Red Guard. His father had given his life to serving his country, and he believed unquestioningly in the goodness of the government.

In an interview with *Newsweek* in 2007, Ha Jin stressed that his family's hardship was not unusual. "There were millions of Chinese in the same situation," he said, many from his own rural town. With their mother away, each brother took on more chores. Ha Jin learned to cook, and soon was responsible for family meals.

Although the schools were closed down, Ha Jin was required to attend study sessions to learn revolutionary songs and dances expressing loyalty to Chairman Mao. Children read from Chairman Mao's *Little Red Book*, a hand-size digest of his famous revolutionary quotations, and spent entire days memorizing passages in praise of Mao and Communism.

Mao's *Little Red Book* was the bible of the Communist state. Here, China's Red Guard soldiers read its verses aloud.

Ha Jin went to the meetings every day, but his mind was elsewhere. Whenever the opportunity arose, he would sneak away to play on the hills and river sides. He liked to sit and watch the sunlight strike the rushing water of the Ussuri River. Because the sessions were not always monitored by party elders, he could usually leave undetected. "I didn't like the activities," Ha Jin said. "I did like fooling around in the wilderness though."

Inside and Out

This image of Ha Jin visiting the Ussuri River, at China's extreme northern border, resonates with his later writing. A main theme in Ha Jin's work is the struggle of the individual to preserve his identity in an oppressive society. In literature, greater freedom is often pursued by the "outsider" character, one who revolts in various ways against authority. In the China that Ha Jin grew up in, however, this option took limited and peculiar forms. One could rebel against one's teachers and enemies of the state, but direct opposition to Chairman Mao's regime could lead to tragic consequences. If one desired freedom, he or she would have to be cunning.

This idea is embodied in the quest of Ha Jin's typical protagonist. Ha Jin has observed that his characters often exist "both inside and outside something at the same time." Characters often seek freedom, yet they must act discreetly, as though they were undercover agents. In Ha Jin's work, freedom is claimed not through direct acts of defiance but rather through personal, sometimes small gestures: falling in love, appreciating natural beauty, educating oneself, displaying humanity to a supposed enemy.

As the Cultural Revolution swept through China, Ha Jin was outwardly a perfect young boy. He went to daily propaganda sessions and pledged his loyalty to Mao's Communist government. He memorized long passages of Mao's essays, shouted patriotic slogans, and adopted the various outward signs of loyalty to the regime. But something else was going on. Playing in the wilderness, Ha Jin was able to carry on a private contact with the world, far outside Mao's gaze.

Military Life

Four years later, war was in the air. Tensions were building on the border between China and the Soviet Union and Ha Jin volunteered to serve in the People's Liberation Army. The Soviets were said to be planning a massive air attack, and Ha Jin did not want to wait idly at home: "Like everyone else, I wanted to be a hero, a martyr." War, Ha Jin believed, would give his life meaning. There were few opportunities for young people at the height of the Cultural Revolution, and his choice was between joining the army and years of labor in the countryside.

Ha Jin has stated in numerous interviews that the most important part for him about being a soldier was protecting the Chinese people: by serving in the army he was countering the violence being inflicted on the public. This is how he viewed his father's service in the army and why he wished to follow in his footsteps. Ha Jin had already seen his mother assaulted, as well as many of his neighbors taken away by authorities. Serving in the People's Liberation Army was his way to help the people.

Besides, the young Ha Jin reasoned at the time, war offered adventure. It promised the kind of raw, exciting experience he wanted so badly, which he had earlier discovered by the rivers and woods as a boy. For Ha Jin and his fellow soldiers, anything—even death—was better than the brutality and numbing conformity of Cultural Revolution–era China. Moreover, joining the army was a great honor at that time. Only thirteen, Ha Jin persuaded his father to use his military connections to allow him not only to enter the army, but also to serve at a young age. Although the minimum age to join the People's Liberation Army was sixteen, Ha Jin was granted early entry.

Border Conflict

The border conflict between China and Russia (then known as the Soviet Union) was a result of the deteriorating relationship between the Communist countries in the 1960s. Although they had been neighbors and allies since after World War II, the Chinese and Soviet leaders had developed a long-standing feud over territory. After the failure of diplomatic talks in 1964, troops began mobilizing along the border on each side.

On March 2, 1969, a group of Chinese soldiers staged an ambush on Zhenbao Island, located between the countries on the Ussuri River, killing an estimated thirty Soviet soldiers. The Soviets retaliated by storming a Chinese stronghold on the river. More than a thousand people died in the battle. Full-scale war between the countries seemed likely, with the Soviets signaling a willingness to use nuclear weaponry.

Ha Jin joined the Chinese army at the peak of the conflict,

In 1969, a border clash between China and the Soviet Union began along the Ussuri River.

early in the winter of 1969. He was immediately assigned the position of artilleryman. In the first winter months, according to Ha Jin, "we were not allowed to take our clothes off when we slept at night, because we had to rush to the front within half an hour if a skirmish broke out." They nearly starved that winter, forced to eat ice-cold turnips from the frozen fields in order to survive. This brutal "turnip-diet" would later appear humorously in several pieces of Ha Jin's first collection of stories, *Ocean of Words*, which recounts his early military experience.

Lost Men

Tensions had reached a fever pitch when something remarkable happened. One day, the soldiers were told that a border agreement with the Russians had been established. There would be no war. For Ha Jin and many of the other soldiers, there was no relief, only a strange feeling of disappointment. "Suddenly I felt really lost," Ha Jin remembered. "We all knew we might die, but most of the soldiers seemed at peace with their fates." Once the expectation of battle faded, a sense of loss prevailed. The men stayed in their garrisons or did drills. They spent long days reading Mao's works, shouting slogans, and writing propaganda in praise of Communism.

Ha Jin was transferred to the local army headquarters where he was trained to send and receive telegraph messages. Once there, he found the kind of darkly funny scenario typical of his later writing. The process of interpreting radio waves was highly challenging, with few men able to handle the painfully sharp frequencies. "It was quite a headache because you had to listen to signals all the time," Ha Jin has recalled. "Some of my fellow soldiers lost their hair—they couldn't get used to that kind of electrical stimulation."

The bizarre atmosphere of bald men coming in and out of the headquarters, shrieking in pain one minute and reciting patriotic slogans the next, made quite an impression on Ha Jin, and this unique blend of cruelty and comedy would later become a hallmark of his writing.

War and Peace

Ha Jin worked as a telegrapher for years until one day a small piece of news changed his world. Someone came into the office and said that Mao had agreed to release a series of classic Chinese novels. To pass the time, Ha Jin began reading one evening. Although he was barely literate, the attempt at reading excited him.

Until then, all that had been available to read was Mao's *Selected Works*, his quotations, and propaganda writings issued by the authorities. Ha Jin went slowly through the first thick paperback text, then faster through the others. "I began to read whatever I could lay my hands on." He would pore over a single page for hours, looking up all the words he didn't know. Gradually, he taught himself to read.

Ha Jin went through many books during that time, but one in particular caught his attention: Russian author Leo Tolstoy's classic novel, *War and Peace*. It was the largest book he had ever seen, and Ha Jin recalled eyeing it nervously for days before finally picking it up. "I was still almost illiterate and could barely read it. But I remember thinking what a revelation this is. I'm here fighting the Russians, and Tolstoy showed that the Russians were just like me."

War and Peace, by the great Russian novelist Leo Tolstoy, made a great impression on Ha Jin, then a fledgling reader with no thought that he, too, might someday become a world-famous author.

This new sense of connection moved Ha Jin and caused him to reflect on his own life as a soldier. For the first time, he began to question the harsh propaganda he had grown up with.

As he entered his sixth year of service, Ha Jin was offered a promotion to ranking officer. The position would have meant greater status and responsibility, but he immediately declined. He had decided to leave the army. Instead, he chose to continue the private exploration he had begun with *War and Peace*. Mao had reopened the schools. Ha Jin would go to college.

Necessity

The well-known saying "necessity is the mother of invention" rings particularly true in charting Ha Jin's unlikely emergence as an internationally acclaimed writer. Ha Jin himself cannot help reflecting on the role that chance, or, as he calls it, "necessity," has played in shaping his life—there is so much that seemed beyond his control.

The random moments that punctuated his youth—his mother taken from home, his chanting propaganda slogans until his voice was hoarse, sunlight on the Ussuri River— were as mysterious as a dream. He could not understand the terrifying logic motivating the Cultural Revolution, and somehow it seemed inevitable and right that he would die at the hands of the Soviets.

Heading into college he had no expectation of studying literature, but rather planned on becoming an engineer. The thought of becoming a writer had not yet taken shape in his mind. Upon enrolling at Heilongjiang University, Ha Jin was asked to list his five preferences for his course of study. "My first choice was philosophy," he remembered. "Then classics, then world history, then library sciences. I didn't have a fifth choice." Without thinking, he jotted "English Studies" down in the last slot.

When he learned the next week that his final preference had been selected by the university officials, he could hardly believe his terrible fortune. For weeks he was miserable. On the first day of school, Ha Jin scored dead last among his peers on a placement exam, a distinction that earned him the frequent teasing of his classmates. "That was humiliating," he recalled. "That's why I never liked English at all."

Worse even than his lowly status, he had an awful time sounding out English words. "I simply couldn't say the words," he said in an interview with the *New York Times*. "I hated English words. They twisted your tongue, your muscles. We all went to the clinic regularly to get painkillers." He plodded through his classes for several years, remaining near the bottom of his class, when one day a stray flyer in his dormitory caught his attention.

A Discovery

The flyer in Ha Jin's dormitory announced an upcoming lecture series on American authors. Ha Jin persuaded several of his friends to come along. The first talk was about the works of Ernest Hemingway and William Faulkner. Ha Jin was fascinated by what he heard. The books being discussed evoked a world far different from his own, full of adventure and wild passions. He immediately went searching for translations of the novels, but found they were not available in China. When he approached a professor who had lectured on F. Scott Fitzgerald, he was surprised to learn that the man, too, had not read Fitzgerald's novels. He told Ha Jin that none of the professors had. They had given their talks based entirely on published reports.

Without access to the actual books, these writers became larger than life in Ha Jin's mind and an aura of mystery was created around them. "The more people talked about the American authors," he said, "the more mysterious they became." His friends joined him in his enthusiasm and soon much of the school was consumed with conversation about American writers who, for all anyone knew, did not actually exist. When at last Hemingway's *Old Man and the Sea* was published in China, Ha Jin and his friends bought several copies each, excitedly reading and rereading their discovery.

Reading Ernest Hemingway's *Old Man and the Sea* (here, Hemingway [*right*] is shown talking to actor Spencer Tracy, who starred in the movie made from his book) led to Ha Jin's decision to study literature in the United States as a graduate student.

Until this point, Ha Jin had struggled greatly with his English studies. Now he had a purpose. He decided he would apply for admission to graduate studies in American litera-ture and began studying feverishly to pass the entrance exam. For weeks after the test he could barely eat, sure that he had failed. Finally, he received word: he had passed by several points. Ha Jin was hailed for his achievement by his class-mates and instructors, who expressed amazement at his rapid academic progress.

Ha Jin began studying for his masters degree the next fall at Shandong University. "Like everyone else," he told the *New York Times* in 2000, "I became obsessed with [William]

Faulkner, with [Theodore] Roethke, with [Saul] Bellow. It was finally okay to read these writers." Ha Jin excelled immediately. But, his thoughts soon turned to more personal matters. He began dating a math teacher at the school named Lisha Bian, and a year later—in 1981— they were married.

As Ha Jin's studies drew closer to the end, his thesis adviser recommended that he continue studying in the United States. In 1985, Ha Jin was admitted with a scholarship to Brandeis University, outside of Boston, Massachusetts. By then, although the Chinese government had relaxed many of its restrictive domestic policies, an official request for permission to leave the country was still needed. Ha Jin's request was granted, under one condition. In order to go to America, he would have to leave his wife and two-year-old son, Wen, behind. By making this arrangement, the government could be guaranteed that Ha Jin would return.

Saddened by his government's decision, Ha Jin decided he would not go to America. Lisha, however, urged him to accept the Brandeis offer. *This is a once-in-a-lifetime opportunity*, she reasoned. *We will be here when you get back*. After weeks of weighing the issue, he took his wife's advice. Packing his bags to leave for the United States, Ha Jin recognized that his life would now be different. Just how much things were about to change, however, he could hardly know.

2

STRUGGLE AND SUCCESS

IN 1985, HA JIN TRAVELED to the United States to pursue his doctorate in American literature. Studying at Brandeis, he began work on the Chinese translations of poets Ezra Pound and T. S. Eliot. His dissertation was aimed at a Chinese job market, and only months into his first year he received an offer from his former school, Shandong University, to teach literature when he returned to China. He called Lisha with the good news. He said he could not wait to be home with her and Wen. "My first years in Boston were very exciting," Ha Jin recalled, "but very lonely. My wife and I wrote many, many letters." In his first months in the Boston area, Ha Jin started writing poems about the mixed emotions he felt about being in America. He would write for hours and then stash the papers in a dusty drawer in his campus apartment. One day, to his surprise, he realized that he had filled the entire drawer.

Smells and Squirrels

"There is a unique American smell that hits when you arrive here," Ha Jin remarked, remembering his first impressions

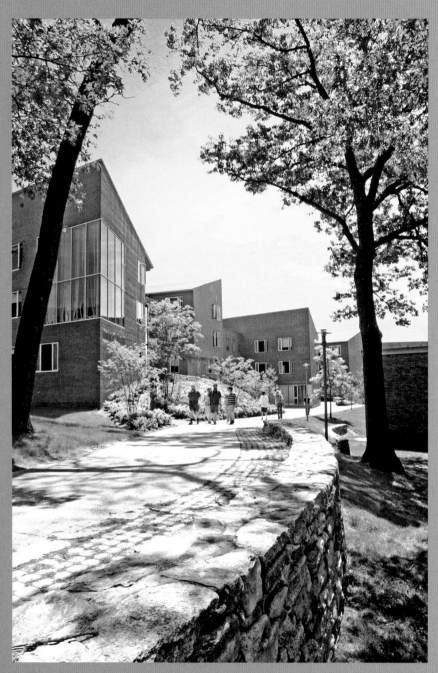
Ha Jin was amazed by the natural setting of the Brandeis University campus.

of the new country. "It is very sweet, like chemicals or a kind of perfume. It makes you sick for a while." He spent his first months at Brandeis with other Chinese immigrants, who all shared their difficulties adjusting to Boston life. One day, they walked down to the Charles River, close to the graduate apartments. Ha Jin was amazed by the beauty of the natural setting. Bright lilies covered the hillside. People lined the shore fishing while sunlight sparkled on the water. Recalling his youthful days by the Ussuri River, his homesickness eased. "Nature has been very generous to the Americans," he wrote a friend back home. "This land is so abundant."

That day, Ha Jin was startled to see people catching big carp and bass fish and then throwing them back into the water. In China, a comparatively poor country, he knew that would never happen. "There were so many squirrels," he has recalled wryly, "and no one was trying to eat them."

The Dead Soldier's Talk

As he continued with his doctorate, Ha Jin's interest in writing poetry blossomed. "I was just dabbling," he noted of these early experiments. He wanted to take a poetry class, but his doctoral obligations prevented him. One day, he approached the poet Frank Bidart and explained his situation. Bidart suggested that he audit a poetry-writing workshop he was teaching at the time and submit work when he could. Ha Jin agreed and prepared a group of poems to bring to the first meeting.

When Bidart read the poems a week later he was astonished. "It was extraordinary to find something this shaped

Poet and professor Frank Bidart was so impressed with Ha Jin's poem, "The Dead Soldier's Talk," that he was instrumental in getting it published.

from someone whose first language was not English," Bidart has recalled. He was so taken with one of Ha Jin's poems, titled "The Dead Soldier's Talk," that he read it over the phone to the editor of the prestigious literary journal *Paris Review*.

The poem was based on a real incident, and was written in the voice of a young Chinese soldier who drowned trying to save a statue of Chairman Mao. Speaking from the grave, the narrator of the poem expresses his devotion to Mao and believes he died for a worthy cause. The poem was immediately accepted. Ha Jin was pleased, but he barely grasped the significance of placing a poem in the internationally renowned journal—on his first attempt, no less.

Only a few days before publication, Ha Jin called the editors and said he had a significant change in mind. When they assured him they liked the poem just fine as it was, he clarified that he meant a change in his name. Jin Xuefei, he believed, would be too difficult for American audiences to pronounce. After talking with Frank Bidart, he decided he wanted something more concise. Recollecting his favorite city in China, Harbin, where he had attended college after serving in the military, Ha Jin reached a decision and, in the process, crafted a new identity for himself. From this point forward, Jin Xuefei Ha Jin would be known as Ha Jin.

Lisha

Despite his success with "The Dead Soldier's Talk," Ha Jin still considered his creative work a sideline to his more important critical research. However, his dissertation on Pound and Eliot had stalled. In addition, his academic scholarship had ended and Ha Jin was forced to work several odd jobs just to survive. Worse, in the winter of 1988 he fell sick with terrible stomach pains and could not write for months. He wrote to the Chinese government asking that Lisha be allowed to fly to America in order to care for him. After several pleading letters, she was given permission to leave, though without Wen. (The government, after all, still needed assurance that Lisha and her husband would return to China.) When Ha Jin saw his wife for the first time in years, he wept with joy. With Lisha at his bedside, he quickly got better and began writing again.

Tiananmen Square

Lisha was preparing to return home when she and Ha Jin were riveted by a drama unfolding on TV. Together they watched as a standoff developed on the streets of Beijing, China. In the large public space of Tiananmen Square, thousands of civilians had gathered to protest the corruption and restrictive policies of the Chinese government. In response, the government ordered the People's Army to take to the streets and disrupt the demonstrations. The people were told to leave the square, but they refused, many chanting in favor of democracy and greater freedom.

Protestors watched helplessly as the Chinese army occupied Tiananmen Square, ending the peaceful student-led protest for democracy.

The conflict took place over a period of seven weeks in 1989. In the last several days, the confrontation escalated. Finally, with the world looking on, the People's Liberation Army was directed to attack the protesters. Hundreds of Chinese civilians were killed, with many more badly injured. Watching with Lisha at his apartment in Boston, Ha Jin was horrified: "I was not mentally prepared for what happened. I had always thought the People's Army was there to protect the people."

Watching the Chinese government brutally murder its own was especially upsetting to the former soldier, Ha Jin, and for weeks he hardly left the house. When Ha Jin was finally able to sort out his thoughts, he realized he could not live under such a regime. He would not return to China. "I couldn't serve a state like that," Ha Jin said. "At the time, all the schools were owned by the state. So any jobs would have been like a state appointment. I had this kind of strong anger."

Ha Jin wrote to the Chinese state department requesting that his son join him and Lisha in America. Ha Jin was amazed to receive a quick answer. Wen had been granted permission to fly to Boston: "In the chaos of the Tiananmen massacre, people just didn't care. He got all the papers." Soon, Wen arrived, having flown alone, uniting the Ha Jin family for the first time in five years.

If Ha Jin had any doubts about his future home, they were erased the moment he saw Wen on American soil. "When he landed," recalled Ha Jin, "I remember clearly that the first thought I had was that he must be an American. That was very clear to me—he must be an American. I didn't want him to be trapped in a cycle of violence and suffering."

Born Writer

Although his commitment to living in America was clear, Ha Jin quickly realized the challenges that would come with his choice. His dissertation had been written for a Chinese market and was little help in finding him a teaching position in the United States. For more than a year he went on a series of fruitless interviews. Meanwhile, he worked odd jobs that only barely provided enough to support himself, Lisha, and Wen. Ha Jin would spend his mornings cleaning houses, nap, and then work all night as a watchman at a chemical plant. He was exhausted and increasingly anxious about the decision he had made for his family.

There was one benefit to the job at the chemical factory: with little to do there, Ha Jin could spend the long nights writing. He began developing the poems he had started when he first arrived in Boston. As he wrote, his fierce anger about Tiananmen found expression on the page. Ha Jin did not feel the writing would amount to much, but Lisha urged him to continue. "My wife encouraged me a lot. She always said, 'You are a born writer, you *must* continue to write." His wife had one consideration, however. "You don't write in Chinese," Ha Jin remembered her saying. "Nobody would accept your writing. You can only do it in English." His wife's words would turn out to be prophetic.

Between Silences

After working at the chemical plant for a year, Ha Jin assembled his handwritten collection of poems and sent them out to the editor Jonathan Galassi, who years earlier had accepted "The Dead Soldier's Talk" for *Paris Review*. Now Galassi excitedly wrote back to Ha Jin and offered to publish Ha Jin's collection, *Between Silences*, through the University of Chicago Press. In the preface to the book, Ha Jin boldly stated his intention to "speak for those unfortunate people who suffered" in recent Chinese history. The subjects of his writing, Ha Jin claimed, were "not merely victims of history. They are also the makers of history. Without them the history of contemporary China would remain a blank page."

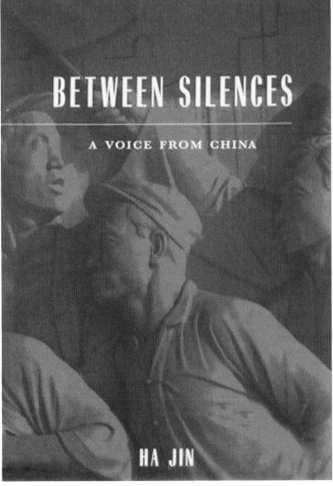

Ha Jin's first book of poetry, *Between Silences*, was meant to give voice to the silenced masses in China.

Survival

Years of uncertainty followed the publication of *Between Silences*. The immediate success of the book had predicted greater things to come, but for some time Ha Jin struggled to find acceptance for his work. Meanwhile, he had no more success finding full-time employment. The enormous challenge of writing in English seemed too great. Ha Jin briefly thought of giving up writing altogether, but again Lisha encouraged him to go forward with his dream. Today Ha Jin reflects that what was really holding him back was the fear of failure. "The real reason for my hesitation was that I didn't know how far I could go. I needed to accept uncertainty as part of the human condition."

Ha Jin began taking classes at Boston University, studying under the novelist Leslie Epstein. The older author encouraged Ha Jin during this difficult period, and Ha Jin has described him as one of his most important mentors. In order to keep his U.S. visa, Ha Jin enrolled as a graduate student in Epstein's fiction-writing program. After little more than a year, however, Ha Jin received the break he had been waiting for. Frank Manley, the director of the Creative Writing Department at Emory University in Atlanta, Georgia, reached Ha Jin by phone and offered him a teaching job. Manley had read *Between Silences* as well as the few stories Ha Jin had published and immediately recognized his potential. Ha Jin quit the program at Boston University and left with Lisha and Wen for the American South and their next adventure.

Ha Jin began teaching at Emory in 1993. It was during this time that he fully committed to a life as a writer. Once more a major turn in Ha Jin's life was driven, at least in part, by necessity. Describing this time Ha Jin said, "I was driven by fear, an instinct for survival. I was hired to teach writing. I had to publish enough to keep my job." Ha Jin realized that he needed to improve his English if he wanted a successful career. Less than a decade earlier he had been at the bottom of his English Studies class at college in China. His development had been remarkable, but he knew he would have to go further. His first several years at Emory, Ha Jin set himself on an intense course of study, essentially relearning the language: "For the initial years it was like having a blood transfusion, like you are changing your blood." As encouragement, he looked to the examples of Joseph Conrad and Vladimir Nabokov, fellow exiles who had learned English later in their lives and gone on to literary greatness. At Emory, Ha Jin would write deep into the night, often falling asleep on a small cot he had set up in the computer room.

By 1996 he had written enough stories to form a unified collection. Encouraged by Frank Manley, he sent them out for publication. After several rejections, his first book of fiction, *Ocean of Words*, was accepted by Random House. Upon its release, the reviews were unanimous: *Ocean of Words* marked the emergence of a major new talent. It had been a long journey, but Ha Jin had finally arrived at his destination. Now there was no holding him back.

HA JIN

Ocean of Words

STORIES

"Extraordinary. . . . [Ha Jin's] laconic, luminous prose makes *Ocean of Words* a nearly flawless treasure."
—CHICAGO TRIBUNE

The stories in *Ocean of Words* draw on Ha Jin's experiences serving in the People's Liberation Army in China in the 1970s.

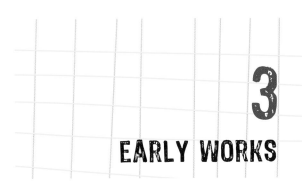

EARLY WORKS

Ocean of Words

WITH *OCEAN OF WORDS* Ha Jin drew on his experiences in the People's Liberation Army to create a hauntingly realistic account of life on the Chinese-Russian border in the early 1970s. The book established a kind of template for Ha Jin's future story collections, exploring a specific time period in Chinese history through a multitude of voices and situations. This kaleidoscopic approach, used later in *Under the Red Flag* and *The Bridegroom*, offers the reader an expansive view of the imaginative worlds Ha Jin creates. In *Ocean of Words*, Ha Jin shows Chinese soldiers desperate for glory and anxious to prove their ideological purity, rival militia leaders obsessed with power, and enigmatic Russian prisoners struggling to escape their shackles.

Throughout the collection of stories, several themes become clear. First, Ha Jin emphasizes the difficult task the Chinese soldiers face in conforming to Maoist ideology. At nearly all times they are suspected by their leaders of being disloyal to the Communist cause. The efforts the men make to prove their loyalty are treated comically in the book, as in the collection's first story, "A Report," in which an officer is forced to apologize to his superiors because his men broke down and cried while singing a revolutionary song. To the military leaders, this show of emotion is shamefully weak and indicates the dreaded "middle-class" values the Communists wanted to destroy. At the end of the story, the officer, fearing reprisal, vows to track down the composers of the song as well as their families and "bring them to swift justice." Here, Ha Jin illustrates how the relentless demands for ideological purity turned the Chinese people against one another.

In numerous stories, Ha Jin reveals the damage that results from the soldiers denying their true thoughts and emotions. Many of the young men in *Ocean of Words* are terribly lonely and long for romantic relationships. In the touching story "Love in the Air," a telegrapher becomes infatuated with a woman he knows only through late-night radio transmissions, but when it is discovered that the woman has parents who were once landowners, he is removed from his position and forced to undergo extensive self-criticism. This process required that Chinese citizens to openly acknowledge their own failures to fulfill the teachings of Chairman Mao, and allowed Mao to keep the public under control by applying cultural pressure. Although the men in these stories never see actual battle, Ha Jin shows that their greatest fight is against their own hearts and minds. The struggle to conform "short-circuits" a number of the men's personalities, driving them to madness.

Ocean of Words won the Hemingway Foundation/PEN award, the highest honor given for an American writer's first book of fiction. *The New York Times Book Review* praised the collection for its "powerful unity of theme and rich diversity of styles." Many critics wondered where this remarkable young writer had come from, and whether Ha Jin would be able to follow up the success of his first effort. They only had to wait one year for their answer.

Under the Red Flag

Ha Jin set his second story collection, *Under the Red Flag*, in the rural Chinese town of Dismount Fort. As in *Ocean of Words*, the stories take place during China's Cultural Revolution and explore the human experience of this painful historical period. While *Ocean of Words* portrayed this subject in terms of individual unhappiness, *Under the Red Flag* is filled with often shocking examples of violence and even perversity. In this collection, an adulteress is stoned and paraded through city streets, a man commits gruesome suicide, and a woman barely avoids being raped.

According to Ha Jin, "My stories are not gentle stories. The question for me has always been, 'How do you write about terrible things without resorting to vulgarity?' I think I might push things farther than people expect. But that's how you test yourself as a writer." Ha Jin's fearlessness as a writer is on full display in *Under the Red Flag*. The book provides a harrowing glimpse into a time in China's history when fear and hatred had spread among the public like a terrible virus. The book won the prestigious Flannery O'Connor Award for Short Fiction, marking a second major honor for Ha Jin only one year after *Ocean of Words*.

Additionally, the lead story in the collection, "In Broad Daylight," won the prestigious Pushcart Prize for best short story of the year.

Turning Point

Ha Jin has described the release of *Under the Red Flag* as a key moment in his literary development. Even after the fantastic success of *Ocean of Words*, he struggled with significant self-doubts. *Under the Red Flag* was published by the highly respected editor Charles East, who had worked with nearly every major American writer of the last twenty years. After submitting his manuscript, Ha Jin waited nervously for a reply.

Finally, he received three pages full of corrections and suggested changes. "I was very embarrassed," Ha Jin said, "and called him to apologize, saying I had worked so hard and I was sorry there were still so many things to fix. Mr. East chuckled and said that this was the first time in his two decades of editing that he had given less than ten pages of notes. There was a long pause as I breathed deeply. That was a real turning point in building my confidence."

Early Themes and Motifs

History and Literature

Ha Jin has stated that one of his main goals as a writer is to put a human face on Chinese history. He grew up during a time when the Chinese people were denied their individual humanity, and in part he has viewed his writing as a way of correcting that injustice. In writing about sweeping historical moments, therefore, Ha Jin has sought to capture the individual stories driving the events: "With history, we have Figures. And Ideas. And Statements. But when you talk about literature, it's about the individuals. How individuals struggle. How individual emotions, ideas, and minds function in the environment." With *Ocean of Words* and *Under the Red Flag* Ha Jin established a style of engaging political subject matter indirectly, through the complex and vivid lives of his fictional characters: "Politics is only a context. The focus is on the person, the inner life, the life of the soul and how that changes."

Life during the Cultural Revolution

In his early stories, Ha Jin emphasizes a unique aspect of Chinese life during the Cultural Revolution. Rather than dwelling on the rampant abuses that the government committed against the Chinese public, he instead shows how, in a climate of fear, individuals turned on each other. This is evident in the story "In Broad Daylight," for example. As Ha Jin portrays an adulteress paraded through the streets by the Red Guard, the most striking development is not what is happening to the adulteress; it is the vengeful attitude that develops among the people watching that day. Ha Jin focuses on a young boy who is drawn out of his house and ends up screaming at the abused woman and throwing rocks at her back. In "Emperor," a group of schoolboys draw from Mao the lesson that power is taken "at the barrel of a gun," and they terrorize their fellow classmates with threats and intimidation. In his first two books, Ha Jin reflected on the way the environment of fear

In his early fiction, Ha Jin showed how the terror inflicted on its citizens by the government and its soldiers also turned civilians—including family members—against one another.

that ruled during the Revolution degraded the common person's decency and sense of compassion.

The Struggle for Freedom

Ha Jin's early work is set during Mao's oppressive Cultural Revolution, a period when direct resistance to state power was futile. One could not simply choose to pose as a rebel or "outsider." An individual who desired greater personal freedom had to fly below the radar, secretly subversive. In Ha Jin's own youth, he discovered a kind of private space during afternoons at the Ussuri River, and later by reading literature as a soldier. This experience is reflected in Ha Jin's early books. In *Ocean of Words* and *Under the Red Flag*, the individual who struggles to exist "both inside and outside" an oppressive society emerges as an archetypal character in Ha Jin's writing. His characters are always searching for that private space in which to exist more freely.

In "Ocean of Words," the title story of Ha Jin's first collection, the main character, a Chinese soldier stationed on the Russian border, seeks freedom through literature. He defies the suspicions of his fellow soldiers and consumes book after book. Other characters fall in love or extend kindness to their presumed enemies. This last idea, one that Ha Jin was first inspired by while reading Tolstoy, is apparent in the story "The Russian Prisoner," from *Ocean of Words*. In this tale, a Chinese soldier who is given the task of guarding a captured Russian soldier develops a covert friendship with the man. Although he must treat the Russian captive as his rival, they develop a bond through sharing small pleasures such as smoking cigarettes, playing Ping-Pong, and eating good food. This story indicates the possibility of friendship across political lines, a theme that would become increasingly important in Ha Jin's later writing.

Love and Sexuality

One of Ha Jin's main interests in his early writing is the consequences of suppressing human emotion. During the Cultural Revolution, citizens were expected to be 100 percent loyal to the Communist cause, and expressions of feeling were generally considered suspicious by authorities. Emotion, like independent thought, could presumably lead people to think for themselves and reject Maoist ideology. This rejection of emotion was especially present in the military environment that Ha Jin grew up in, and in which the stories in *Ocean of Words* are set.

The most common way that Ha Jin approaches the theme of suppression is through love relationships. Frequently in these stories, characters develop romantic feelings for the opposite sex that they are required to deny. Some, like the lead character in "Too Late," risk everything and run away with their lovers. However, more often Ha Jin's soldiers attempt to discipline their true feelings. Ha Jin shows how this act of denial leads to perverse sexual acts such as rape, having sex with animals, and even castration. With no positive outlet for their natural desires, Ha Jin's soldiers act out in any number of bizarre ways. These violent sexual acts fill Ha Jin's early work, depicting a culture that denies the place of love and honest emotion.

Comedic Surface

One of the distinguishing features of Ha Jin's writing is his blend of satiric humor with often tragic subject matter. "I want to be truthful to life," Ha Jin said. "In reality, no matter how grim and sad life is, people who live it still find a way to amuse themselves and make life more bearable. I want to give my work a comic surface, but in essence the stories are tragic." Ha Jin's tragicomic style emerged fully one year after *Under the Red Flag*, with his first novel, *In the Pond*.

In the Pond

Released in 1998, *In the Pond*, Ha Jin's first novel, suggests a great deal about the work that would bring him fame in the coming years. A brilliantly satiric tale, *In the Pond* begins with an epigraph from the classic Russian writer Gogol that states in part: "Alas, after all's been said, I still can't choose a virtuous man as my hero. . . . Now I feel the time has come to make use of a rogue." Gogol was known for his use of the "trampled" Russian common man as his literary protagonists in various works, and in choosing this quotation, Ha Jin reflects a similar intention.

Ha Jin chose a poor, disrespected Chinese factory worker named Shao Bin as his protagonist. With his choice of Shao, Ha Jin returned to his original goal as stated in *Between Silences*, to elevate the "poor and unfortunate" Chinese citizenry in his writing. In all respects, Shao makes an unlikely hero. He is average in his intelligence, frequently rude in his manners, and a lazy employee. There is, however, one characteristic that sets Shao apart from his fellow workers: he is a talented painter who dreams of successfully pursuing his art.

In the novel, Shao, a factory worker at a fertilizer plant, is being passed over for a new apartment by the commune leaders at Dismount Fort. Shao is newly married and has been waiting patiently for a larger apartment for years. When he investigates, he discovers that he was in fact in line to receive the apartment, but was ignored in favor of friends

Chinese workers, most likely similar to Ha Jin's character Shao Bin, load bags of fertilizer onto tractors outside of a fertilizer plant.

of the party's leaders. Shao approaches the leaders of the plant and explains his case, but he is mocked and laughed out of the room. In retaliation, Shao paints a large political cartoon mocking the commune leaders as corrupt and inept. Although he hangs the painting anonymously in the factory, word quickly spreads that Shao is the artist responsible and he is swiftly punished.

The novel follows a similar narrative pattern. Shao desires to attend college on an art scholarship, but the plant leaders declare him insane and attempt to stand in his way.

As the corrupt leaders attempt to repress his challenge to their authority, Shao must decide whether to relent, or pursue his dream of becoming an artist. In the end, he risks everything in order to fulfill his dream and succeeds in escaping the oppressive compound. The final image of the novel shows Shao ecstatically leaving the noisy factory. Ha Jin writes: "On his way to the Commune Administration, he couldn't resist smiling and whistling. In the sky a flock of geese were drifting south and gradually merging into the cotton clouds. Joyously Bin stretched up his right arm, as if he too had wings."

The Value of Art

In the Pond develops the key idea in Ha Jin's work of art as a vital expression of freedom. In fact, the journey that Shao Bin undergoes in the novel offers a clear parallel with Ha Jin's own literary story. For both Ha Jin and his underdog protagonist, art offers a way of defining meaning within a frequently absurd or degrading political system. In his 2008 essay "The Language of Betrayal," Ha Jin reflected on his unlikely emergence as an artist and clarified several past statements often cited by critics. He wrote:

> I have been asked why I write in English. I often reply, "For survival." People tend to equate "survival" with "livelihood" and praise my modest, also shabby, motivation. In fact, physical survival is just one side of the picture, and there is the other side, namely, to exist—to live a meaningful life. To exist also means to make the best use of one's life, to pursue one's vision.

For Ha Jin, writing had begun as a way of seizing meaning from the senseless tragedy of Tiananmen Square. At the time, he spoke of wanting to give meaning to the lives of his fallen countrymen, but looking back, he could see that it was also his own life, his own dreams and fears, that needed articulation. For years he struggled in poverty, learning the English language so that one day he could write freely. It seems fitting that *In the Pond* was the last book Ha Jin wrote in relative obscurity. The novel's final image of the perennial underdog Shao Bin ready to soar into the bright sky could equally have applied to Ha Jin himself. The following year he would achieve his breakthrough with *Waiting* and soar higher than he could have dreamed.

WAITING

WINNING AMERICA'S PRESTIGIOUS National Book Award, *Waiting*, published in 1999, brought Ha Jin international acclaim and a suddenly expanded reader-ship. The novel was Ha Jin's first love story and surprised many critics who had grown accustomed to the intensity and wartime setting of his earlier stories. Although different from his earlier work in both tone and storyline, *Waiting* develops Ha Jin's previous exploration of the human impact of the Cultural Revolution. In the story of a repressed middle-aged man unable to find true love, Ha Jin created a powerful commentary on the struggle of the Chinese people to find happiness during this traumatic historical period. True to his style, *Waiting* avoids overt political commentary, choosing to portray history through the vivid inner lives of his characters. The novel brought Ha Jin a feeling of security after years of struggle. As he stated, "After *Waiting*, I could finally breathe."

Plot

Waiting begins with a prologue and then is organized into three parts of twelve chapters each. The story is told from

Ha Jin won the 1999 National Book Award for his novel *Waiting*.

the third-person perspective with the narrator giving us access only to the thoughts of Lin Kong, the main character. The simple, elegant structure of the book has been compared to that of a fable, and helps draw the reader in through its engaging approach.

Prologue

Waiting begins by introducing the basic premise of the novel. Every summer, Lin Kong, a doctor in the Chinese army, returns to his rural home in Goose Village to seek a divorce from his wife, Shuyu. Each year, for many years, Shuyu agrees, only to change her mind at the last moment. In the prologue to *Waiting*, Shuyu and Lin make the annual trip to Wujia Town to see a marriage judge. Lin is hopeful that this will be the year that Shuyu keeps her word and the divorce is certified. He has promised Manna Wu, his girlfriend at the hospital, that this time he will return to the city a free man. At last they will be able to live openly together, without secrecy or shame.

Before they leave for Wujia Town, Ha Jin briefly sketches Lin's relationship to Shuyu, introducing an important theme in the novel: the transition from "Old" to "New" China. The most significant detail we receive about Shuyu concerns her bound feet, a cultural tradition that by 1983, when the book is set, had become rare. "This was the New China," Lin thinks, "who would look up to a young woman with bound feet?" Lin is ashamed of his wife and no longer loves her. Ha Jin writes: "[Lin] felt that the family didn't depend on him anymore and that it was time to move along

Doctors were not exempt from being treated as elements of propaganda by the Chinese Communist state.

Among the few things Ha Jin tells us about Shuyu, the wife of Lin, the hero of *Waiting*, is that she has bound feet like the woman pictured above.

with his own life." This tension between individuality and collective responsibility, tradition and modern values, runs throughout *Waiting*.

Shuyu's brother, Bensheng, tags along as they head to Wujia Town for the divorce court. Once in the court, it is Bensheng who speaks forcefully against Lin, claiming that Lin is being cruel by attempting to divorce Shuyu. Bensheng emphasizes that Shuyu cared for Lin's sick parents during their time of need. The judge agrees, denouncing Lin as "immoral and dishonorable," and demanding to know whether he has a conscience or not. For the seventeenth straight year, the divorce request is rejected.

When Lin returns to the hospital, Manna, a nurse who is Lin's girlfriend, is devastated to hear the result of his trip. "Another year?" she exclaims. "How many years do you have in your life?" Lin urges her to be patient. The following year will mark the eighteenth of Lin's separation from Shuyu. According to Chinese law, after this time an officer can end his marriage without his wife's consent. The scene ends without resolution. As a fellow nurse comes upon them, Lin and Manna part ways. Ha Jin finishes the prologue by emphasizing the limitations placed on Lin and Manna's relationship. Hospital rules dictate that unless a man and a woman are married or engaged, they must not be together outside the compound. Lin and Manna cannot venture past the brick wall surrounding the building. This image of confinement resonates throughout the book, as Lin and Manna struggle with their growing love for each other.

Part I

At the start of Part I, *Waiting* shifts back in time to the beginning of Lin and Manna's relationship. Manna is heartbroken because her first love, Mai Dong, has just ended their engagement. Although she's only twenty-seven, she fears that she will soon be thought of as an "old maid," like two other unmarried women at the hospital. Lin and Manna first meet during a training mission. The Cultural Revolution is beginning and the government organizes the Chinese public for possible conflict. After days of training, Manna's feet become badly blistered and Lin comes to her aid.

The following chapters describe Lin and Manna's evolving romance. Ha Jin writes of Lin: "His life had been simple and peaceful until one day Manna changed it." Manna is determined to make an impression on Lin and leaves tickets to the theater on his desk one day. When Lin arrives, he is surprised to find Manna in the seat next to him. During the show, they lock fingers. Lin is surprised by Manna's boldness, but does not resist her advances. He begins to feel strongly for her, deciding, "If this leads to an affair, so be it."

Soon Lin and Manna begin spending more time together. During an early walk, they discuss joining one of two organizations associated with the Cultural Revolution and Maoist propaganda. Manna is interested in joining, but Lin argues against doing so. "You don't have to fight with others to be an active revolutionary, do you?" Here, as throughout the novel, Lin's impulse is toward independence.

Lin's feelings for Manna grow into love. "It was the first time that he suffered such a longing to be with a woman," Ha Jin writes. Their relationship, however, is threatened by the judgments of others. Lin and Manna seek privacy, but soon they find themselves the subject of gossip in the hospital. The vice-director of the hospital's Political Department calls Lin into his office one day and warns him against pursuing an "abnormal" relationship with Manna. When people in the hospital begin to complain about Lin's lifestyle, Lin decides to end things with Manna. "We will be treated like criminals," he tells her. Manna responds that she does not care.

If she hadn't gotten embroiled with a married man, Lin's girlfriend Manna might have been one of these carefree-seeming nurses photographed during the Culture Revolution.

Lin attempts to suppress his desires for Manna. "As long as he kept himself busy," Ha Jin writes, "he felt in control and self-sufficient. He needed no woman." At a dinner celebrating the National Day holiday, Lin can't take his mind off Manna. He watches her laughing and enjoying the company of several men at a nearby table. Instinctively, Lin approaches to warn her against drinking too much, but Manna only smiles, replying mockingly, "Am I drinking anything that's yours?" As the table dissolves in laughter, Lin feels humiliated, and he leaves the party. Outside, however, Manna catches up to Lin and declares her love for him.

She challenges him boldly: "Are you a man or not? You have a fearful heart like a rabbit's." Lin determines to try again for a divorce that summer.

Lin returns to the country to ask for a divorce. Yet, after spending a week with Shuyu, he feels again that he cannot ask for a divorce. For the first time, he understands how lonely his wife must be. When Lin returns to the city, he finds that Manna has lost patience. She demands to know what Lin plans to do. Lin reasons that they should break off their romantic relationship. "No matter how we love each other," he states, "there'll be no chance for us. Better to stop before we're trapped too deep."

Lin's words infuriate Manna. "What will become of me?" she cries. "It's easy for you to say that—to be so rational. Don't you know the whole hospital treats me like your second wife? Don't you see that all men here shun me as though I were a married woman?" Where Lin's instinct is toward being coolly rational, Manna's is toward following her heart. In addition to developing this contrast, here, as elsewhere in *Waiting*, Ha Jin emphasizes the societal pressure placed on Lin and Manna's relationship, particularly noting the judgment and disapproval that Manna is subject to. "Everyone was supposed to marry," Ha Jin writes, "even the retarded and paralyzed were not exempt."

Part II

At the beginning of Part II, Lin receives a letter from his cousin, Liang Meng, asking for help in finding a girlfriend. Lin decides to set Liang up with Manna. Although Lin admits that Manna is the only woman he has ever had deep feelings for, he is disturbed by what could happen to both him and Manna if they continue their relationship. Their careers could be ruined. Ha Jin writes: "In many people's eyes, the two of them had already become near-pariahs involved in something illegitimate."

Manna agrees to meet Lin's cousin, but on their first date discovers they have no chemistry. The next day at the hospital, Manna tells Lin the date went poorly. To Lin's embarrassment, he feels a surge of delight at hearing this news. Manna agrees that she is not disappointed her date went so poorly. "If I only I didn't love you so much," she says. The directness of her expression moves Lin. Manna holds Lin's hand and tells him not to try to set her up again. With the summer approaching, Lin resolves to try again for a divorce.

At the courthouse, the judge is close to granting a divorce when Shuyu breaks down sobbing. She states that she still loves Lin. The judge demands to know if Lin has a mistress, but Lin insists he does not. The judge does not believe him and dismisses the case. Outside the court, an angry mob has assembled, waiting to attack Lin if he wins a divorce. Their leader is Bensheng. He has rallied the entire rural community against Lin. For the people of Goose Village, Lin's attempt to get a divorce marks him as an enemy to their traditional values.

The next day, Lin is stunned to find a story about his divorce case spotlighted in the local newspaper. The author of the piece attacks Lin for "betraying" his marriage vows. Soon after this most recent court hearing, Lin is paid a visit by his older brother, Ren Kong. Ren scolds Lin for trying to divorce Shuyu, who, after all, has been so good to the Kong family. He urges Lin to forget about Manna. Back in the city, a request is made by party leaders for Manna to go on a date with the military commander, Commisar Wei. With Ren's words echoing in his head, Lin does not attempt to stand in the way. Reluctantly, Manna agrees to the date.

Manna's date with Wei goes well. He asks her to read Walt Whitman's book *Leaves of Grass* and send him a letter with her thoughts. She agrees. They end their date by attending the theater, where they watch a melodrama praising China's military greatness. There, Manna is introduced to Wei's friend, army officer Gene Yang. During the play,

American poet Walt Whitman was revered in Communist China as a kindred spirit, though he would have shuddered at the thought, had he been alive and aware of his fame there.

many people, including Wei, are moved to tears, but Manna notices that Gene Yang sits stoically throughout. Afterward she speaks to Yang and asks him how he could not have been touched by the scenes on stage. Unexpectedly, Yang recounts a tale of a group of his soldiers being accidentally buried during a routine training exercise. He speaks of meeting the grieving parents: "I had to remain coolheaded in order to maintain discipline among my men. One by one I turned down the parents' unreasonable demands . . . so many men die in accidents; a man's life is worth nothing."

At Manna's request, Lin helps Manna with her reading of Whitman's book of poetry. Manna copies his notes in her own writing and mails the letter to Commissar Wei. Soon after, Lin falls ill with tuberculosis. While quarantined in the hospital he is paired with a roommate who is known as a legendary warrior in the military. The man turns out to be Gene Yang. The two strike up a friendship. As Lin relates his situation with Manna, Yang encourages him to act boldly. His resolution to Lin's dilemma is to take Manna as a mistress. "What's the good of being a *good man*?" he asks. He chides Lin: "You know so much, but you can't act decisively." Lin weighs his advice carefully.

With Lin out of town visiting the country, Manna notices that she doesn't miss him very much. One night she visits Lin's room at the hospital and Gene Yang answers the door. He reeks of alcohol. After some small talk, Yang begins to press himself forcibly on Manna. Despite her attempts to fight him off, Gene Yang rapes Manna. Ha Jin emphasizes the gap in power between the two. Afterward, Yang tells Manna, "You can go tell anyone you want. Who will believe you?" Manna hesitates to take the incident to the hospital authorities: "Won't they say I offered myself to him?"

Manna debates what to do. Her friend, Haiyan, discourages her from pressing charges, telling her that in China a rape is rarely treated as a rape. Worse, women are usually thought to be at fault. Haiyan continues: "This has happened to a lot of women. In fact, my elder sister was raped by a friend of hers some years ago, and she couldn't do anything about it."

When Lin returns, he is shocked to find Manna very ill and much thinner than before. Manna struggles with feelings of anger toward Lin for introducing her to Gene Yang. She withdraws from him. Finally, after several weeks, she tells Lin the truth of what happened. Lin comforts Manna, but is concerned that she has told Haiyan about the incident. "If this gets out," he tells her, "you'll have a personal catastrophe. People can kill you with their tongues." This statement reflects the power of societal judgment and the intense pressure to conform in Cultural Revolution–era China.

Soon Lin's concern is realized. Word of Manna's rape spreads across the hospital and Manna is subjected to cruel taunts: "The curses often made Manna feel as though she had lost a limb or a vital organ and become handicapped. How she regretted having divulged the secret to Haiyan." The combination of these terrible events brings Manna closer to Lin. Ha Jin ends Part II by flashing forward to 1984. After eighteen years of separation, Chinese law allows Lin to divorce Shuyu with or without her consent. Lin asks Shuyu to come to the hospital to—at last—legalize their divorce.

Part III

Part III begins with Shuyu's arrival in Muji City. She experiences extreme back pain, the result of years of working in the fields, and must rest at the hospital. The nurses ask her many questions about her relationship with Lin, wondering if he treats her well. Shuyu insists he is a good man and states that she harbors no bitterness over their situation.

Voiceless for most of the novel, Shuyu becomes a more prominent figure in the final section. After resting in the hospital, she receives a haircut in the city that gives her a stylish new appearance. Lin wants both Shuyu and his daughter, Hua, to move to the city, believing they will have more opportunities there. Lin writes to his daughter, asking her to come immediately. He realizes with shame that it is the first time he has sent her a letter.

At the courthouse the next day, Lin is finally granted a divorce. Lin is amazed at how quickly the lengthy process has come to an end, and he feels that he is about to turn over a new page in his life. To his dismay, Hua writes back that she is not interested moving from the country. Lin returns to Goose Village to see his daughter in person. He is saddened to see the bond that has formed between Hua and her uncle, Bensheng. Lin feels jealous, realizing his own relationship with his daughter has suffered. After spending several days in the country, Lin and Hua grow closer. She agrees to return to the city with him.

In the city, Lin helps Shuyu and Hua get settled, buying cooking items and furniture for them. Hua begins working at a match plant in town. Once they have fully moved into their new place, Lin focuses on planning his wedding with

Manna. The wedding is a quiet affair, reflecting the guests' mixed emotions toward Lin and Manna's relationship. At one point during the reception, a guest approaches Lin and Manna somberly. "Love and take care of each other," he tells them. "Don't forget that yours is a bitter love." He repeats the words "bitter love." After he leaves, Manna begins to cry, and Lin steers her away from the crowd and comforts her. Though Manna leaves, Lin stays until the final guest has left, alone and bored. The wedding is a disappointment, foreshadowing a growing ambivalence about their relationship that both Lin and Manna begin to feel.

Once married, Lin feels that he cannot keep up with Manna's passion and intensity. At the hospital, his fellow workers tease him for being too old for Manna and Lin snaps back angrily. At one point, Manna tells Lin: "I don't know why I feel so sad. If only we had married twenty years earlier." Although Lin is unsure of her precise meaning, he also expresses a similar disillusionment later: "Sometimes Lin thought about the twenty years before this marriage. He couldn't help imagining what this home would have been like if Manna and he had gotten married fifteen years earlier."

Soon Manna is pregnant. Lin urges her to have an abortion but Manna affirms her independence, stating, "I want my own baby." When Hua and Shuyu learn of the pregnancy, they are happy. For Shuyu, this is a great event, because it means that their family will now be larger. Lin doesn't understand this sentiment, even wondering if this meant Shuyu thought they were still married. However, soon Lin begins to respect Shuyu's positive attitude about their divorce.

Manna gives birth to twin boys, as Lin grapples with a complex mix of feelings. He wavers between pride and sadness. Seeing the young lives, he reflects on the passage of time. Ha Jin ends chapter eight with the poignant comment:

> Lin felt weak and aged; he was unsure whether he cared for the twins and whether he would be able to love them devotedly. Watching their covered faces, somehow he began to imagine trading places with them, having his life start afresh. If only he himself had been carried by someone like this now; then he would have led his life differently. Perhaps he never would have had a family.

In the weeks after giving birth, Manna's health deteriorates. Forced to take care of both his wife and twins, who cry at all hours of the day, Lin too is miserable. He hires a nurse to help around the house. One day she takes the boys outdoors in freezing weather and they become sick. The diagnosis is dysentery. With the twins ill, Lin feels their suffering as his own, and realizes for the first time he truly loves them: "For the first time in his life he was experiencing this kind of paternal suffering, which caused him to tremble a little."

The doctors at the hospital are unable to help the boys. Lin and Manna begin to feel hopeless. It appears that their twins will die. Hua comes to visit and shares Shuyu's advice on curing dysentery, an "old-world" remedy of taro, sugar, and egg yolk. Although Lin and Manna are doubtful it will work, they are desperate and give it a try. Miraculously, it cures the twins of their painful illness.

One night, the new show *To Get Rich Is Glorious* appears on TV. The program reflects the emergence of capitalism in China. As Ha Jin writes: "A few years ago their ways of making money had been illegal, but now the noveaux rich were held up as examples for the masses to follow." While Lin and Manna are watching, the show spotlights Gene Yang, who has become rich running a construction site. Manna is terrified and has nightmares for weeks.

Manna's health continues to weaken, and the doctor tells Lin she will die within a few years. Manna becomes extremely irritable, and she and Lin have a terrible fight. This leads Lin to question whether marrying her was the right thing to do. He realizes he has never been able to give his heart fully to another person and is consumed with sadness.

Lin goes into the city to visit Shuyu and Hua. After drinking several glasses of liquor, he at last opens up emotionally, telling Shuyu tearfully, "Sweetheart, I didn't mean to hurt you. Can, can you forgive me?" This is the first point in the novel where Lin shows his true feelings. Shuyu accepts his apology and tells Lin she is happy he has come to visit. Lin says that he is a bad man, but Shuyu rejects his words.

Hua comes to visit Lin and Manna the next day, caring for the twins and helping them decorate their apartment. She tells Lin how happy his visit the previous night made Shuyu. Outside the room, Lin hears Manna wishing someone "Happy Spring Festival," sounding cheerful and full of life. Lin feels comforted and realizes that his new life might be a blessing after all. Finally, he feels prepared to face the future.

Themes and Issues
Confinement

A major theme throughout *Waiting* is Lin and Manna's inability to openly express their feelings for each other. At the beginning of the novel, Ha Jin states that they cannot go out in public together beyond a low wall encircling the hospital, and this sense of confinement pervades their lives. In the China of Ha Jin's book, there is no place for Lin and Manna's love, both literally and metaphorically. They cannot take their relationship outside the walls of the hospital, and are increasingly threatened even inside their place of work. As word spreads about their relationship, they cannot do anything without quickly becoming the focus of malicious gossip.

Ha Jin has commented on the loss of privacy that characterized Cultural Revolution–era China, where *Waiting* is set. During this time people had to worry constantly that their own neighbors would inform on them to the Red Guard. "Your banker would tell your neighbors how much money you had in your bank account!" Ha Jin recalled to the *New York Times*. "It was something you didn't even question." This atmosphere pervades *Waiting*, as Lin and Manna struggle to find a safe space to be together.

Throughout the novel, Ha Jin characterizes their relationship in terms of a desire for openness. Manna reasons that marriage would be good for her and Lin because, "it might provide an opportunity for a couple to talk and listen to each other, since they wouldn't dare speak their minds in public." Shortly after, she again wishes for a room of her own, where "she could cry to heart's content and yell at the top of her lungs without being heard by others."

Suppression

By suppressing his feelings for Manna, Ha Jin shows that Lin becomes emotionally closed off, unable to respond empathetically to either Manna's or Shuyu's situations. While home visiting Shuyu, Ha Jin writes of Lin: "Her words made him realize that his wife must have been lonely when he was away. He hadn't thought she had her own ideas and feelings."

Lin's inability to grow emotionally close to Shuyu and Manna—in fact, to anyone—is a strong theme throughout the novel. One day Lin discovers old love letters from Manna's first boyfriend, Mai Dong, and is shocked at the young man's passion. Lin feels conscious of his own emotional disconnect, reflecting that he had never experienced such intense emotion for a woman.

For Lin and Manna, the tragic result of living under an oppressive society is that they internalize the need to deny their feelings. This leads each of them to great unhappiness. At this climactic moment of *Waiting*, Ha Jin returns to the image of confinement: "It occurred to him that the rule that prohibited two people of the opposite sex from walking together outside the wall had been abandoned. Yet somehow to him and Manna, there still seemed to be a wall around them."

Sexuality and Power

In *Waiting*, Ha Jin explores the consequences of a culture that denies the place of love and honest sexuality. The pressure on Lin and Manna to suppress their feelings for each other drives each of them to unhappiness. Throughout the book, Lin grapples with feelings of shame over his desire for Manna. "I can control my desire," he tells himself at one point.

However, despite Lin's best attempts to repress his emotions, he is unsuccessful. Ha Jin demonstrates this at the end of chapter eight through a vivid dream of Lin's in which he has intercourse with an unnamed woman in an open field. He is one with nature and with his own sensual self. In other words, Lin's yearning to live freely and his desire for Manna are one and the same. During the dream he climaxes. The next day he urgently tries to wash his bedsheet without anyone noticing but his secret is discovered by a coworker. Lin feels ashamed and responds angrily to the man's teasing.

For Manna, the consequences of her sexual desire for Lin are more serious. At the beginning of the novel she is shown as a confident, modern woman comfortable with her own sexuality. Manna reflects the Communists' principle of gender equality that was a main part of Mao's ideology—at least in theory. She initiates flirting with Lin, and is the first to propose that they have sex. However, at the same time, Ha Jin describes the pressure she is under to deny her love for Lin. When news of their relationship gets out, she is teased for being Lin's "second wife." Her sexual life becomes fodder for gossip at the hospital; other women are particularly cruel toward her. Most tragically, after she is raped by Gene Yang, she is demeaned as a "slut" by the other women, and treated as an outcast within her community. In his characterization of Manna, Ha Jin shows how, despite the supposed progress brought on by the Communists, women were brutally punished for being independent and confident with their own sexuality.

Family

Throughout the novel Ha Jin uses the theme of family to explore the conflict between individuality and traditional values in China. In his attempts to divorce Shuyu, Lin pursues an individual path that causes both Bensheng, Shuyu's brother, and Ren, Lin's own brother, to rebuke him. Both men denounce Lin for subverting the traditional Chinese value of family. Although Ren appears only briefly in the novel, he plays an important role in the development of this theme.

After greeting Lin early in the second part of the novel, he immediately takes him to task for attempting to divorce Shuyu, "She's given everything to our family," Ren states, reminding Lin that it was their parents' wish that they marry. Lin responds coldly that it was their wish that "messed up my life." Lin insists that this is his personal matter, yet Ren sees it differently. "A divorce will affect everybody in our family," he tells Lin. "Kids in my village have already started calling your nephews names, saying 'your uncle has two wives." Ren's visit weighs heavily on Lin, yet Lin ultimately rejects his brother's concerns and continues his pursuit of Manna.

Characters

Lin Kong

The main character of *Waiting*, Lin Kong is a married doctor in the Chinese army who at the beginning of the novel begins an affair with an educated nurse named Manna Wu. In one of our first glimpses of Lin, he is asked to join a group of female nurses at dinner. He declines, fearing he would become the subject of gossip if he accepted, but Ha Jin writes:

"If only he could have eaten dinner with the nurses in there. He wouldn't mind walking twenty miles just for that." This image of loneliness characterizes Lin, as he struggles to find inner happiness.

Over the course of the book, Ha Jin follows Lin's eighteen-year quest to divorce his wife, Shuyu, and live freely with Manna. Although Lin is a gentle man who does not wish to harm anyone, he is unable to fully empathize with the circumstances of either Shuyu or Manna. At key points in the book, Lin admits that he has not understood the depth of pain that Shuyu and Manna have experienced. Lin is an emotionally distant man who only understands his need for others at the end of the novel.

Unlike his brother, Ren, Lin values individual freedom over the obligations of family. He chafes against his arranged marriage to Shuyu and curses his parents for "messing up his life." He recoils from Shuyu largely because of her bound feet, which to him represent an embarrassing feature of China's past. Above all, Lin desires independence. At the time of the Cultural Revolution, when the novel takes place, this proves a difficult goal. Lin is an outsider, not because of his desire to divorce his wife, but also because he is an intellectual who must hide his books from hospital authorities, and who is even told to change his hairstyle at one point because he looks too much like a "bourgeois liberal." Lin's independent nature is further seen in his refusal to join citizen groups promoting Mao's Cultural Revolution. Early in their relationship, Manna presses him to join a group with her, but Lin responds forcefully: "They just waste their time arguing and fighting. You don't have to fight with others to be an active revolutionary."

His desire to divorce his wife makes him an outcast in his home village. In the city he is treated with a measure of respect and acceptance, yet even there he must hide his true feelings for Manna. This constant suppression takes a painful toll on Lin. Over the course of the novel he withdraws emotionally and questions his ability to love. When Shuyu at last grants him the divorce he has been waiting for, he finds his marriage to Manna is not what he hoped it to be. Lin is a complex character who reflects Ha Jin's interest in the emotional and mental toll that Chinese culture inflicts on the individual.

Shuyu Kong

The first time we see Shuyu Kong, it is through the eyes of her husband Lin. Observing his wife at their rural home in Goose Village, "he was dismayed—she looked so old, as if in her forties, her face wrinkled and her hands leathery." Lin feels no love for Shuyu, instead thinking of her as a "cousin." For much of *Waiting*, Ha Jin reveals little about Shuyu. When she speaks, it is only with a few words, or a nod or shake of the head. She is defined mainly as a loyal wife, mother, and caregiver. It was Shuyu who cared for Lin's parents in their later years. Although Lin appreciates her generosity, he notes that his parents died long ago. As his love for Manna develops, Lin grows increasingly impatient with Shuyu and steps up his efforts to win a divorce.

Shuyu's attitude toward the possibility of divorce is complex. Each year she agrees to Lin's wish, only to change her mind at the last moment. When the judge asks her if she still loves her husband, she answers honestly that she does. Shuyu is presented as a simple woman who is incapable of lying. Much of the novel explores China's transition into modernity, and Shuyu's function in the novel is largely as an embodiment of an old culture that is being left behind. Ha Jin connects Shuyu to the past through the image of her bound feet, a traditional practice increasingly rare in the contemporary China of the novel. The physical pain that Shuyu suffers because of her feet reflects her broader sacrifice for her family.

In the final third of the novel, Shuyu emerges as a surprisingly strong character. When she finally accepts the divorce with Lin she harbors no bitterness. Indeed, it is Shuyu who has the deepest insight into Lin's marriage to Manna, insisting to a confused Lin "the family just got bigger." Lin cannot understand her response, but this attitude reflects Shuyu's deep commitment to family, and abiding love of Lin. Ultimately Shuyu's support is instrumental in helping Lin and Manna through the difficult first months of their marriage. After one newborn falls terribly ill with dysentery, Shuyu alone provides a cure. Her old-world treatment is mocked at first by the modern doctors caring for Lin and Manna's son, but to everyone's surprise it brings the twins back from the brink of death. By the end of the novel, Shuyu has emerged as a powerful figure, guiding Lin towards the inner peace that has eluded him.

Manna Wu

Manna Wu is an educated nurse at the army hospital in Muji City where Lin also works. While Shuyu represents China's old-world culture, Manna reflects the modern ideal of womanhood suggested by the Communists during the Cultural

Revolution. The Communists believed that women and men should have equal rights, and Manna's confident and energetic personality reflects this new role. The first time we see her, she is laughing freely and playing a vigorous game of volleyball. Manna is assertive, even bold about pursuing what she wants. She initiates the relationship with Lin and, throughout the first half of the novel, urges him to claim his love openly and to leave Shuyu behind. Increasingly, Manna grows frustrated with Lin's indecisiveness.

Despite her desire for independence, Manna is frequently constrained by the judgments of others at the hospital. In this respect, Ha Jin indicates the limitations of the push for women's rights during the Cultural Revolution. Within the hospital, Manna is a constant focus of gossip and demeaning comments. While being courted by Lin, she is viewed as his "second wife." Later, she is the envy of the women at the hospital when she is pursued by powerful military officer Commissar Wei. Ha Jin writes: "Manna was aware that people began treating her differently. The hospital leaders became very considerate to her. Every now and then a nurse would fasten meaningful eyes on her, as if to say, 'Lucky girl'."

Gradually, Manna's wish for independence is undercut by those around her. After she is raped by military commander Gene Yang, she is told that no one will believe her, and she is urged to keep quiet. When word of the attack gets out, she is scorned by her fellow workers in the hospital, who view her as a "broken" woman and even a "slut." In the final stages of the novel, Manna's physical and mental health deteriorates. She grows increasingly unhappy, even as Lin finally divorces Shuyu to be with her. After the rape, she is never the same. Our initial impression of Manna as energetic and boldly confident is overturned completely by the end of *Waiting*. Manna is a tragic character who reflects both the enthusiasm that followed takeover by the Communists, and the eventual bitterness and disillusionment of the Cultural Revolution.

Gene Yang

Military Commander Gene Yang appears at the halfway point of *Waiting*, and plays a pivotal role in the remainder of the novel. Manna first meets Yang while at the theater with Commissar Wei. She is struck by his stoic and rough demeanor. While nearly everyone in the theater is in tears by the end of the performance, Yang remains unmoved. When Manna asks him why he tells her that he has seen terrible things in the army and no longer becomes emotional easily. He recalls having to report the deaths of his soldiers to their grieving loved ones. "So many men die in accidents," he tells Manna, "a man's life is worth nothing."

Initially, Ha Jin presents Gene Yang as Lin's opposite. Where Lin is calm and rational to a fault, Yang is aggressive and decisive. After learning of Lin's situation with Manna, Yang urges him to boldly pursue a divorce. "See, you know everything," he says mockingly, "but nothing can make you steel yourself. If you really have the will to change, you can create the conditions for change." Yang's personality appeals to both Lin and Manna, and they confide in him about their struggles to forge a relationship. Manna particularly admires Yang's blunt manner, and wishes that Lin could acquire the more forceful aspects of his personality.

Although Lin and Gene Yang seem quite different, they have more in common than first appears. In a sense, both are victims of the oppressive social environment that existed during China's Cultural Revolution. Ha Jin has described Lin as "emotionally crippled," and the same could be said of Yang. As Lin is unable to express emotion, Yang has lost all sensitivity and human compassion as a result of his military experiences; he has become hardened, a monster. This is clear from his reaction to the theatrical performance early in the novel, and then later in his rape of Manna. His act of rape is the most violent and disturbing moment in the novel.

At the end of *Waiting*, Yang appears on TV flaunting his newfound riches on a show called *To Get Rich Is Glorious*. This scene is a darkly ironic take on China's early embrace of capitalism, suggesting a new opportunity for individuals such as Yang to exploit the Chinese people.

Bensheng

Shuyu's brother, Bensheng, is Lin's rival throughout *Waiting*, standing in the way of his repeated attempts to divorce Shuyu. Each year, Bensheng accompanies his sister to the divorce hearings, arguing for the judge on her behalf. Early in the novel, he tells the judge that Lin is being unfair. "He can't treat a human being, his wife, like an overcoat," he says, "once he has worn it out, he dumps it." Time and again, Bensheng's words persuade the judge to deny Lin's request for a divorce. Gradually, Bensheng's manner toward Lin grows more hostile.

After scuttling an early divorce attempt, Bensheng remains friendly toward Lin, sharing his hope that they are still "one family" despite their differences. Later, however, Bensheng rallies support in Goose Village against Lin. The next time that Lin and Shuyu go to court, an angry mob wielding knives and pitchforks waits for Lin outside the building.

Bensheng's attitude toward Lin reflects the depth of the emotional response in Goose Village. Many in the rural town view Lin's desire for independence as selfish and damaging to the community. Moreover, Lin's desire for divorce suggests the broader changes occuring in the country at the time. The Cultural Revolution was a period of great upheaval, and Bensheng's anger at Lin reflects traditional Chinese culture desperately trying to hold on to the old way of life.

Literary Reception of the Novel

Upon the release of *Waiting* in 1999, critics hailed the novel as Ha Jin's greatest achievement. As the reviews poured in from around the world, it was clear that Ha Jin had reached a new milestone in his career. The *New York Times Book Review* wrote that "*Waiting* provides a crash course in Chinese society during and since the Cultural Revolution," while the *Chicago Tribune* described the novel as "a simple love story that transcends cultural barriers, filled with an earthy poetic grace." Despite the stream of positive reviews that greeted *Waiting*, Ha Jin was unprepared for the run of awards that followed the novel's release. *Waiting* won both the National Book Award and the PEN/ Faulkner Award, considered America's top honors for fiction. In addition, the book was a finalist for the Pulitzer Prize.

While Ha Jin had already established a dedicated readership, the astonishing success of *Waiting* brought his writing to a far wider audience. The novel shot to the top of the *New York Times* best-seller list, where it stayed for nearly a year. For a time it seemed that *Waiting* would be Ha Jin's first book made available in China, yet at the last moment the Chinese government denounced the novel and warned Ha Jin's prospective Beijing publisher not to release it. Because no official reason was given by the government for their last minute decision, Ha Jin was perplexed. "Maybe it's because I have been very outspoken about the Tiananmen massacre," he said. "The government, of course, doesn't like that. So perhaps it is because of me as a person rather than the book."

PULITZER PRIZE FINALIST

"Powerfully moving. . . . Brilliant and original. . . . Timeless and universal. . . . Nearly perfect." —Russell Banks, *The New York Times Book Review*

WAR TRASH

Winner
PEN/FAULKNER AWARD

a novel

HA JIN

NATIONAL BOOK AWARD-WINNING
AUTHOR OF *WAITING*

War Trash, a novel about a Chinese prisoner of war in Korea, is considered one of Ha Jin's two masterpieces.

WAR TRASH

WAR TRASH, released in 2004, is considered Ha Jin's second masterpiece, equal in stature to *Waiting*. Set during the Korean War, the novel tells the story of a Chinese soldier captured by American forces and held for years as a prisoner of war (POW). Throughout the book, he must navigate a complex web of pressures in order to survive and reach his goal of returning to his girlfriend and family in China. The novel revisits several of Ha Jin's favorite themes—the dangers of nationalism, the struggle for freedom, and the possibility of harmony between rival groups—while creating a story of powerful universal appeal. *War Trash* was awarded the PEN/Faulkner for best book of fiction in 2004 and was also nominated for a Pulitzer Prize that year.

Plot

War Trash is organized into thirty-six short chapters that move briskly from one scene to the next. The novel is narrated by Yu Yuan, a former officer in the Chinese People's Liberation Army, who recounts his experiences as a prisoner of war held by American forces during the Korean War. The novel unfolds like a memoir, with Yu leading the reader from the outbreak of war to his final release back to China.

Part I (Chs. 1-12)

In a brief prologue, the narrator of *War Trash*, Yu Yuan, introduces himself to the reader. Now an elderly man living with his grandchildren in Atlanta, Georgia, he describes his plan to write the story of his experiences during the Korean War. Speaking with his grandson, he states his wish that by writing his story he will help prevent future wars. He urges his son to go into the medical profession, which he describes as being far away from "political nonsense" and full of "compassion and human decency."

Yu begins his story in 1949, with the onset of the Communist takeover in China. He is a young college student in love with his fiancée, Julan. The country is full of optimism at the political change. Yu shares this sentiment, writing, "I felt grateful to the Communists who seemed finally to have brought peace to our war battered land." Engaged to be married in the coming year, Yu "had never been so cheerful." However, soon Yu is assigned to the 180th Division of the People's Liberation Army, and by 1951 his unit is sent to fight in the Korean War. Tearfully, he says goodbye to his mother and Julan, who breaks a jade barrette and gives half to Yu as a pledge of her love. Yu vows to return for them.

In these early chapters, Ha Jin introduces a main theme of the novel: Yu's gradual disillusionment with the romantic notions of war. He and his fellow soldiers are told that there will be little resistance from the Americans, yet soon his division encounters a bombed village, the land reduced to rubble. Yu remarks that, until then, "I hadn't been able to imagine the magnitude of the war's destruction." Ha Jin emphasizes the soldiers' feeling of betrayal by their leaders. In a key early scene, a wounded Chinese soldier wails simply, "They lied to us! They lied to us!"

Shortly after, the Chinese are surrounded by Korean and American forces. Their supply lines are cut and the men go for days without food. Commissar Pei, the leader of Yu's

North Korean and Chinese Communist prisoners of war sit together on the ground at a United Nations POW camp during the Korean War.

division, considers a retreat, but before he can decide to do so he is ordered by superiors to conduct another offensive. Pei resists, claiming that such a mission is futile, but he is overruled. The attempt to break out of the encirclement fails, and Yu's division is cornered. The next day, a grenade attack levels Yu's group, and Yu is captured as a POW.

In the prisoner camp at Pusan, Yu attempts to hide his identity. He gives a false name and does not reveal that he can speak English. His left thigh has been fractured in the attack, and he initially refuses treatment because he does not trust the American doctors. Yu relies on his ward mate, Wanlin, to feed him and help him relieve himself.

Yu develops a friendship with a female American surgeon, Dr. Greene. This helps him overcome his instinctive hatred of Americans. He begins to realize that the anti–American propaganda he has been taught is not always true. As Yu begins to trust Dr. Greene, he reveals his actual identity. Dr. Greene shows sincere compassion for Yu and helps nurse him to better health. In a sign of their budding friendship, the doctor asks Yu for lessons on how to write Chinese characters. Told that he must leave the next day to go to a POW camp on Koje Island, Yu is sad to part with Dr. Greene.

Approaching the huge camp, Yu is overwhelmed with anxiety and loneliness. The new compounds are "as big as city blocks," and he is separated from his friend Wanlin. His compound is controlled by pro–Nationalist Chinese and he is pressured immediately to accept passage to Taiwan. He is told that soon there will be a screening during which he will be forced to choose between Taiwan and China. The

Nationalist leaders of the compound assume that anyone resisting the call to go to Taiwan is a Communist, and those who resist are threatened with violence and given little food. However, Yu insists on his desire to return to China. His reasons are not political, but rather personal. His motivation is simply to see his family and fiancée again, and this goal sustains him in his fight to survive.

The next day, Yu learns that someone from the Communist camp has betrayed Commissar Pei. After Pei's identity is revealed, he is captured and tortured. Ha Jin highlights the different responses that Yu and the other men have toward the assault on Pei. While Yu is more concerned with Pei's health, others in the camp on the Communist side demand revenge. They set their sights on Yu's old friend, Wanlin, whom they believe informed on Pei. Soon, Wanlin is discovered dead after a brutal beating. When Yu challenges his fellow Chinese POWs about their action, they justify the act by claiming the party must not tolerate dissent. Yu is shocked at the willingness of his fellow soldiers to elevate abstract principles above their humanity.

As the screening approaches, Yu is taken in for questioning and accused of being a Communist. The Nationalists reveal that they know his true identity. In front of several hundred Nationalists, Yu is pressed to reject Communism and accept going to Taiwan. However, again he refuses. "I'm not a Communist, Chief Wang," he tells the Nationalist leader. "I want to go home only because I miss my mother and fiancée." Eventually, Yu is allowed to leave the meeting. But on his way home he is surrounded and assaulted by Nationalists. They knock Yu unconscious. When he wakes he sees he has been left with a tattoo across his belly that reads: "F*** Communism." This makes it nearly impossible for Yu to fulfill his dream to return to China, which depresses him. He instantly starts thinking of ways to remove the tattoo.

As he weighs the impending screening, the Nationalists step up their efforts to intimidate the Chinese POWs. Liu Tai-an, a violent Nationalist leader on the island, orders them together for a frightening "pre-screening." Tai-an urges the men to cut their ties to the Communists, and he demands to know each prisoner's decision. Only one soldier, Lin Wushen, is bold enough to declare his intention of returning home. In a shocking scene, Liu disembowels the dissenter in front of the entire gathering. Another avowed Communist is viciously beaten. At last, seeing no other way, Yu and his friend Dajian decide to go to Taiwan. On the day of the screening, however, security is surprisingly relaxed. They see an opportunity. After telling the guard that he will join the group heading to Taiwan, at the last moment Yu slips onto the boat to China. His daring move succeeds, but Yu feels ashamed at leaving his younger friend behind.

Yu is taken to Compound 602, a settlement of 4,000 run by Chinese Communists, thus known as the "Mainland Compound." He is warmed by the sight of the Chinese flag flying openly and quickly greets his old friend, Commissar Pei. As Yu observes the many maimed and disfigured Chinese soldiers, he begins to grasp the true devastation of the war. Seeing these men, "wearing eyeshades to cover their empty eye sockets, who had lost their hair, ears and noses to napalm," Yu realizes they have no choice but to return to China—no one else would want them.

With the Chinese in leadership positions in the compound, the United Communist Association is formed to build power. Despite his conflicted feelings toward the Communists, Yu decides to apply for membership in the association. He is surprised to find, however, that his application is turned down. Yu is looked at with suspicion because of the assistance he gave an American pastor, Father Woodworth, on Koje Island, and his earlier friendship with Dr. Greene. Yu undergoes self-examination. "They made me feel like a traitor under interrogations," he remarks bitterly. He is told that he will have to prove his loyalty to the Communist Party.

Part II (Chs. 13-25)

Yu is given the important job of translator. Each day he reads the American newspapers and passes on important information to Commissar Pei. He is asked to always consider the morale of the Chinese soldiers, and Pei urges him not to tell anyone that Chairman Mao's son has been killed in an air raid.

As the Communists consider Yu's party application, they force him to complete a risky loyalty test. Yu is made to steal an American GI's gun while the man is sleeping. He is very anxious about completing this task, but because of his desire to return to his family in China, he pushes forward, bringing an iron bar along in case he needs to defend himself. As the man sleeps, Yu successfully steals his weapon. On the way out of the man's room, however, he accidentally drops the bar. To Yu's horror, the Americans recover the evidence.

The next day, the Americans descend on the Chinese camp with the metal bar, demanding to know what happened. When no one confesses, they detain a group of POWs and return them the next day, badly beaten. Yu is given a citation for bravery by the Communists, an important moment in his inclusion in their ranks.

A meeting is requested by the leaders of the North Korean POW compound, with whom the Chinese are in frequent contact. Commissar Pei sends Yu and another man to attend. At the meeting, Mr. Park, the leader of the North Korean POWs, reveals a plan to capture General Bell, one of the Americans' top commanders. The goal is to create an international incident that will draw attention to human-rights abuses committed by the Americans. Pei is concerned about the repercussions of provoking the Americans, but he agrees to support the tactic, ordering his men to go on a hunger strike immediately. While the strike continues, a letter is sent demanding changes in living conditions, repatriation, and a meeting with General Bell.

At the meeting in the Korean compound, General Bell listens patiently to the soldiers' complaints and says that he will see what he can do to help. Bell states that he respects his Chinese and Korean adversaries. Likewise, Yu reflects that "to me, he seemed like an honorable man." The different parties return to their respective compounds, with the Chinese continuing their hunger strike.

The next week, Yu is summoned again to meet with the Koreans. As they arrive they see a big sign declaring that General Bell has been abducted, and American military personnel surround the compound. A "Truth Conference" is set for the next day, with Bell forced to stand trial in front of his captors.

At the conference, General Bell is confronted with evidence of his men abusing and torturing North Korean POWs. The condemnations, some from survivors of torture, continue for several days. When it is Yu's turn he shows his unwanted tattoo and proudly declares his national loyalty: "Let me tell you, if we're alive, we're Chinese men; if we're dead, we're Chinese ghosts." For the first time in the novel, Yu truly feels a part of the Communist cause. The next day, General Bell signs the declaration that admits to mistreatment of the prisoners, and agrees to improved conditions in the future.

The Chinese consider Bell's admission a major propaganda victory, and Yu is praised for his role in the success. However, shortly after Bell is released, the agreement is revoked by the Americans. In the coming months, they step up their harassment of the Chinese soldiers. The Americans begin an offensive against the Chinese and North Korean camps, killing dozens. Yu is taken into custody and briefly tortured. At night, he hears the pained screams of his fellow soldiers.

While in his cell, Yu sees an American lieutenant with whom he has been friendly. The man approaches Yu and denounces him for taking part in the abduction of General Bell, claiming that the Chinese humiliated a "good family man." Yu does not disagree that Bell was a good man, but is surprised to hear the lieutenant speak in such personal terms. For Yu, the capture of General Bell was not a personal matter. In one of *War Trash*'s most significant passages, Yu reflects after the man has left: "This is the crime of war: it reduces real human beings to abstract numbers." Yu remembers Dr. Greene and wishes that, like her, he could see soldiers as individual people, not as statistics in the horror of war. As the leaders of Compound 602 prepare for an assault against the American forces, Yu senses his enthusiasm for the "collective struggle" waning. He begins to doubt the logic of the abduction and feels that he has been used by the Koreans.

The Americans order the Chinese POWs to accept a transfer to a compound organized by the Nationalist Chinese, on Cheju Island. Commissar Pei believes the intention is to separate the Chinese from their Korean allies. Pei and Yu debate whether to fight the transfer. Yu is impressed with Pei's prudence in deciding against armed resistance. "I don't want to get our men into danger," Pei states. American troops force them out of the compound, marching six thousand Chinese soldiers down to the shore.

Once there, the Americans threaten to seize Commissar Pei. In a sign of Yu's new standing among the Communists, he is asked to speak on behalf of the Chinese. Yu tells the American leaders that the Chinese won't board the ships unless Commissar Pei comes with them. Suddenly a voice rises up from behind Yu shouting, "We won't board the ship!" which thousands of Chinese prisoners echo in unison. The Americans relent, allowing Pei to board the ship with them. The Chinese POWs are sent to Cheju Island and Yu is given a second citation for bravery.

On Cheju, the prisoners initiate a "Study Movement" meant to redouble their ideological commitment to Communism. They read texts from Mao and work to improve their reading and writing skills. The prisoners seek a way of communicating with Commissar Pei, who is sequestered in a cell miles from their compound. After being placed in a nearby prison for a minor offense, Yu joins with his two cell mates in devising the "Pei Code," an elaborate system (like an alphabet) that allows them to communicate undetected with their leader. Soon, the men are released and return to their compound with valuable information: Commissar Pei has ordered the men to celebrate National Day of the People's Republic of China on October 1 by raising the Communist flag. The act is meant to demonstrate the prisoners' resolve and fighting spirit. Pei urges the soldiers to prepare themselves for battle in the event that the Americans resist their celebration.

The next days are spent making daggers and machetes, as well as constructing the flag itself. Yu worries that a massacre is about to take place. There is no way their limited tools can match the American artillery. Yu questions his comrades' loyalty to a flag above the possibility of a significant loss of life. He grows to reject the Communists' habit of placing abstract ideas over human life.

Although he fears the upcoming fight, Yu comes to understand the complicated motives guiding his fellow prisoners. "We all felt ashamed of becoming POWs because we should have died rather than submit to capture. Many even believed our captivity had impaired our country's image." Just before National Day, a prisoner informs the Americans of the Chinese plan. The Americans search the six compounds and assault those holding weapons. With the

Chinese prisoners in disarray, a message is sent from Commissar Pei urging them to go through with the plan. The night before National Day, Pei's lieutenant rallies Chinese POWs with the cry, "Defend our national flag with our blood and our lives."

U.S. Marines stood guard on January 19, 1954, on the road liberated anti-Communist POWs were to travel from Panmunjom. Next to them was a sign reading "Friends, this way to Freedom Bridge."

Yu is horrified by what he sees as the impending suicide mission, and he questions Pei's motives. The next day the Americans come and demand the Chinese take down their flag. A bloody battle is waged and more than fifty Chinese men die. Another hundred are seriously wounded. Despite these tremendous losses, Commissar Pei declares the fight a "glorious victory" and awards each man in Yu's battalion a medal for bravery. Yu realizes that the distribution of medals is fraudulent and feels disgusted with himself for not seeing this sooner.

Part III (Chs. 25-36)

Yu learns the true reason for Pei's reckless endangerment of his own men. His goal had been to start another propaganda campaign to embarrass the United States. As Yu remarks, "The more people got killed, the more sensational the event, and the more reverberant the victory would be." Realizing this, Yu feels sick to his stomach. He believes that the war has changed Commissar Pei for the worse. Moreover, Pei's attempt to win international sympathy fails. No one pays any attention to the slaughter of the Chinese POWs. The next day, the Chinese are punished with hard labor.

Yu wishes to join the men in the difficult work, but he struggles because of his injured knee. The other POWs tell him that they would rather Yu not join them. Even after all of his contributions to the Chinese resistance, Yu is still not accepted as a Communist. At this late point in the novel he no longer feels a need to be accepted, having earlier stated outright that he doesn't believe in the ideology. Both Yu's distance from Communism and his status as an interpreter place him in a kind of border territory between the Communists and Nationalists, the Chinese and Americans. Even more than his long-suffering comrades, Yu is truly alone.

The Chinese are informed that four of their officers must return to Pusan to re-register with American officials. One of the men called upon is Chang Ming, Commissar Pei's personal interpreter. The mission is risky and Pei feels that Chang Ming is too valuable to go. Instead, Yu is ordered to pose as Chang Ming and travel to Pusan in his place. Thinking about his family, Yu gives in to his emotions and breaks down sobbing. He writes a letter to be given to his girlfriend, Julan, in the event that he dies. Several of Yu's friends in the compound throw a going-away party for him. Boarding the boat for Pusan the next day, Yu does not recognize the three men sailing with him.

Back at Pusan, Yu wonders if Dr. Greene still works in the camp hospital. His memory of her remains as strong as ever. At registration, Yu's fingerprints do not match those of Chang Ming and the officials realize he is an impostor. To Yu's surprise they do not immediately punish him, but rather attempt to gain information about his plan. Yu is so angry with Pei that he tells the truth, stating "Chang Ming is Pei's interpreter, indispensable to him. That's why Pei sent me, to be trashed." This statement is significant, for here we see the image of "war trash" evolving. Now, like his fellow POWs, Yu recognizes that he too is viewed as "trash" by the Chinese leaders.

The American officers question why Yu would continue to associate with the Communists, given how they have treated him. They urge him to accept passage to Taiwan. Yu reiterates the motivation he has stated throughout the novel: he feels no particular allegiance to the Communists but simply wants to return home to his family. "I'm my mother's only son," he tells the interrogator. The Americans refuse to allow him to return to the Communist camp. With no other choice, Yu accepts his ultimate transfer to Taiwan. Before he can leave for Taiwan, however, he must wait in a Nationalist-controlled camp near Cheju Island. As he leaves Pusan, Yu thinks he sees Dr. Greene and rushes up to a woman who is walking away from him. When she turns around, however, Yu realizes sadly that she is a complete stranger.

After he has spent several months in the Nationalist camp, the armistice is signed, ending the Korean War. The prisoners are elated, but Yu remains uncertain. He still dreams of returning to China, but he has begun to lose hope. Yu also fears what may happen to him and his family if he does return to China. It is widely thought that the POWs will be received as traitors who have disgraced their nation. Moreover, Yu believes that his association with the Nationalists will make him a particular target. At this late point in the novel, Yu still has not reached a decision—there seem to be no good options.

Word arrives that, before the men are sent to Taiwan, there will be one final screening known as "The Persuasion." The Communists will make one last attempt to coerce the prisoners to return to their natural home. In preparation for the screening, the Nationalists wage a week-long propaganda campaign against the Communists, including a radio address by Nationalist leader Chiang Kai-shek promising the prisoners that they will be treated as heroes if they relocate to Taiwan. As The Persuasion approaches, Yu struggles greatly with his choice.

Finally, the day arrives. Yu is stunned to see that his old friend from the beginning of the war, Chaolin, is his questioner. Chaolin greets him warmly. Yu shares his concern about returning to China, but Chaolin firmly asserts his support: "I shall always stand by you. It was the Party that sent you to Pusan, and you won't be blamed for the consequences. You made a great sacrifice, Yuan. Nobody will blame you." Yu is moved by Chaolin's words and at last decides to return home. In the final chapter of the book, Yu describes his difficult reentry to China. Along with the other POWs, including Commissar Pei and Chaolin, Yu undergoes extensive self-criticism sessions in which he is forced to accept blame for disgracing his country.

Worse, Yu is devastated to learn that his mother has died, and that his girlfriend, Julan, has abandoned him. Yu had wanted to marry as soon as possible, feeling overwhelmed with a new appreciation for the value of human life. Yet this is not possible. Julan's brother confronts Yu and explains that she couldn't possibly marry a "disgraced captive." The POWs are treated as the lowest members of Chinese society and no one wants to be associated with them.

Yu is surprised to find that Commissar Pei is treated no better than the other former prisoners, despite his high rank. As Yu states bitterly, "He too was war trash." With few exceptions, the men are dishonorably discharged by the military. Many express regret that they risked so much to come home to fulfill their idea of loyalty. Yu is spared a worse fate by Pei and Chaolin, who stand up for Yu and exonerate him of conspiring with the Nationalists. Yu is grateful for their friendship, which he had not realized was so strong. Pei also helps Yu change his tattoo from an anti–Communist slogan to one which condemns the United States.

After losing Julan, Yu spends many years alone, choosing the life of a bachelor. Over time, however, this bitterness fades. "Life continues," Yu states, "despite our personal misfortunes." Yu falls in love again and starts a family. His son is accepted to university in the United States, and Yu becomes the grandfather of two American children.

Themes and Issues
Horror of War

In *War Trash*, Ha Jin emphasizes the way all sides—Chinese, Korean, and American—are degraded by battle. Ha Jin uses a Chinese narrator, Yu Yuan, and so, at the beginning of the novel, the reader may instinctively feel sympathetic to the Chinese forces. As early as the second chapter, however, the Chinese capture an American soldier and badly torture him. This shocking moment comes directly after Yu expresses his amazement at the carnage he has witnessed in the first days of fighting. "I hadn't been able to imagine the magnitude of the war's destruction," Yu states. "Around me, men hollered and moaned, and some were twisting on the ground screaming for help." Throughout the novel, Ha Jin shows that the true horror of war is the loss of moral conscience that occurs among the soldiers. Although the reader might understandably be more sympathetic to the Chinese, Ha Jin underlines that this loss affects each side equally. By making this point, Ha Jin denies the propaganda of war, which defines the opposing forces as evil and therefore unworthy of human dignity.

The Value of the Individual

At a key moment in the middle of *War Trash*, Yu questions his superior, Commissar Pei, for leading his men into a battle that will undoubtedly lead to massive Chinese casualties. Yu comes to realize that Pei is willing to sacrifice his men in order to win a "propaganda victory" against the American forces. Alarmed by this realization, Yu reflects, "This is the crime of war: it reduces real human beings to abstract numbers."

This moment with Commissar Pei marks a turning point in Yu's evolution as a character. At the beginning of the book he participates eagerly in the war, convinced it will be an adventure that will bring honor to his country. He believes that the Communists have changed China for the better and throughout much of the novel he yearns to be a part of the larger collective struggle. Shortly before his encounter with Pei, Yu had expressed pride at being useful to the Communist cause. After helping in the plan to kidnap General Bell, Yu states, "I felt for the first time that I was a useful man, and that my life had finally been shaped by a goal." After his conversation with Pei, however, Yu's commitment to the Communist struggle begins to wane. He starts to realize a key idea in *War Trash*—that individual lives must be valued over ideological goals. This attitude contrasts starkly with that of the governments involved in the war, which treat the soldiers merely as "war trash."

The Dangers of Nationalism

In writing about the Irish struggle for independence in the early twentieth century, poet W. B. Yeats wrote that, "The best lack all conviction, while the worst / Are full of passionate intensity." With this statement, Yeats expressed his belief that the people who believed most avidly in the cause of independence were, in a sense, the worst, because they were willing to commit violent acts in order to achieve their ends. A similar idea is expressed in *War Trash*. Ha Jin demonstrates that the military leaders on each side of the Korean conflict were able to manipulate the soldiers through nation-

Mao Anying, the eldest son of Mao Zedong, was killed in action during the Korean War. His statue was unveiled sixty years later, in commemoration of his death and as a sign of nationalist pride.

alistic appeals. Ha Jin shows that the belief in the superiority of one's nation, be it Chinese, Korean, or American, leads to hatred, ignorance, and violence.

The central irony of *War Trash* is that, despite the nationalist appeals that fill the novel, the Chinese soldiers are treated the worst by their own country. Simply due to their status as POWs, they are thought to have brought shame and disgrace to their country. The Chinese soldiers remark throughout the novel that they would have preferred death to captivity. They know that if they do manage to survive and return home, they will be treated as the lowest of the low in society. Indeed, this fear is realized when Yu finally returns to China at the end of the novel. He finds that his fiancée, Julan, wants nothing to do with him. Her brother warns Yu to stay away from her, describing him as "filth." The cruel irony of the soldiers' situation is that once they are captured, everything they have fought for is instantly proven a lie. Rather than being heroes in their country, they are discarded as "war trash" and left without a true home.

Common Humanity

In *War Trash*, Ha Jin contrasts the senseless brutality of war with a belief in the common humanity among people of different races and cultures. This theme is first presented in Yu's friendship with Dr. Greene, but occurs throughout the novel, highlighting Yu's development as a character. After Yu has been injured at the beginning of the book, it is the American, Dr. Greene, who cares for him in Pusan. Yu initially refuses treatment, passionately declaring that

Americans are his enemies and cannot be trusted. His relationship with Dr. Greene, however, affects Yu profoundly. As they get to know one another, Yu is surprised when Dr. Greene insists that she cannot hate the Chinese. Eventually, they develop a bond; Yu teaches her Chinese calligraphy as a gesture of gratitude for her medical care. When Yu leaves Pusan, Dr. Greene writes a note to the American forces excusing Yu from hard labor due to his injury.

While at the beginning of the story Yu echoes the Communist Party conviction that Americans are enemies of the Chinese, he gradually sees that he and the Americans are similar in many ways. After arriving at the Koje Island POW camp, he grows close to an American guard named Richard. The men smoke cigarettes together and one day begin talking about their girlfriends back home. When Yu breaks down and cries, Richard comforts him, saying, "It's tough, man. I know it's tough." One day Richard tells Yu, "I don't see why I'm here. Fighting for what?" a sentiment expressed by Yu and other Chinese soldiers elsewhere in the novel. As their bond grows, Yu writes Richard a "Safety Certificate" that will protect him in case he is captured by Chinese forces. This act of friendship is similar to the note that Dr. Greene wrote on Yu's behalf at the end of chapter four.

Later in the novel, there is a violent clash in the compound between the Americans and Chinese. A young Chinese boy is chased by a GI, but at the last moment, Richard intervenes and protects the boy. This act of kindness saves the boy's life. Throughout the novel, Ha Jin suggests that despite their political differences, the men fighting on different sides of the war have a great deal in common.

The Power of Knowledge

One of the most important subplots in the novel involves Yu's attempt to learn English. On Koje Island, he begins attending church services and borrows a Bible from the church pastor, Father Woodworth. For Yu, learning English is an act of resistance. "The words of the Bible made me giddy," Yu reflects, "simply because it was not propaganda." Yu's plan to learn English meets great resistance from the Communist leaders, however. Soon, Yu gains a reputation as a "bookworm" and is lectured for his "deviant" behavior. When his superiors find out that he has borrowed a copy of the Bible, Yu is isolated from the rest of the soldiers and forced to perform a series of loyalty tests. It is clear that to the military leaders that populate *War Trash*, the most dangerous weapon a soldier can have is an educated mind.

Throughout the novel, Ha Jin links the pursuit of knowledge to humankind's powerful desire for freedom. This is seen later during the "Study Movement" that arises among the prisoners of Cheju Island. With their morale at its lowest point, the Chinese prisoners dedicate themselves to learning how to read and write. Yu acts as one of the teachers; his favorite student is a young soldier named Shanmin. After being tortured badly at the hands of the Americans, Shanmin has lost all desire to live and has become nearly mute. Working with Yu, however, he begins to stir to life. Each day, Yu teaches Shanmin ten words. One day, Yu is shocked to see that Shanmin can read an entire article in a Chinese newspaper. The two develop a strong friendship that lasts until the end of the novel. Observing the amazing progress of Shanmin and many other Chinese prisoners, Yu exclaims, "How mysterious, tenacious, and miraculous life could be!" In *War Trash*, the thirst for knowledge demonstrates the resilience of the human heart in the face of tragedy and horror.

Characters

Yu Yuan

The narrator of *War Trash*, Yu Yuan, is studying political science at the Huangpu Military Academy when he is called to fight in the Korean War. Yu is not a member of the Communist Party but is given an important position in his battalion because he can speak and write English. This unique status makes Yu an outsider within his unit as the war begins. He is distrusted at first not only because he is not a Communist but because he is an intellectual in a culture hostile toward liberal education. Yu's desire for knowledge raises the suspicions of his military superiors, and yet ultimately this trait wins him the respect of his fellow soldiers.

Other characteristics mark Yu as an outsider in the People's Liberation Army. In contrast to most of his fellow soldiers, Yu lacks ideological conviction. Because he is not a Communist, he is able to see the good and the bad in the Nationalists, Koreans, and Americans. Thus, Yu demonstrates the shallowness of military propaganda and the common humanity uniting all sides of the war. Rather than having a strong political motivation, Yu is driven by his love for his family. Throughout the many trials he endures in the novel, he is sustained by the desire to return to his mother and fiancée, Julan. Although he is repeatedly offered safe passage to Taiwan, Yu risks his life in order to return to China. Ha Jin uses Yu to demonstrate that within the apparatus of war, soldiers themselves were often peaceful and shared similar desires to be with family and loved ones.

Dr. Greene

The American physician Dr. Greene is a highly significant figure in the novel. She is introduced in chapter four, when she treats Yu's leg injury after he is struck by a grenade. Yu is initially hostile to the American medics in the POW compound at Pusan, but soon develops a friendship with Dr. Greene. Yu is impressed with Dr. Greene's kindness and compassion. In an important conversation between them, she surprises Yu by stating that she does not consider the Chinese to be her enemies. She shows an interest in learning more about Chinese culture and asks Yu to give her lessons in calligraphy. Yu begins meeting with her regularly until he is transferred out of the camp. When it is time for Yu to leave, Dr. Greene gives him a pen as a token of friendship, which Yu holds onto dearly over the course of the novel. Near the end of the novel, Yu returns to Pusan and hopes to reunite with Dr. Greene but cannot find her.

For Yu, Dr. Greene serves as a symbol of human decency and goodness that survives amid the hatreds of war and political propaganda. Yu comes to believe that doctors represent the best in humanity, and he urges his grandson at the beginning of the novel to pursue a career in the medical field. Although she only appears in a single chapter of *War Trash*, Dr. Greene has a profound effect on Yu and influences his evolution over the course of the novel.

Liu Tai-an

Liu Tai-an is the vicious leader of the Chinese Nationalist forces that control Compound 72 on Koje Island. Ha Jin uses Tai-an to demonstrate the powerful divisions that existed in China after the Communists had taken power from the Nationalists. Yu and his fellow POWs fear Liu Tai-an and the Nationalists even more than the Americans. On Koje Island, Tai-an demands that the Chinese soldiers cut their ties to the Communists and join the POW group relocating to Taiwan. In order to achieve his goal of returning home to China, Yu must navigate not only the American forces, but the Chinese Nationalists as well.

In another way, Liu Tai-an reflects a central theme of the novel. In *War Trash*, Ha Jin makes an effort to strip away the false romance of war, and bluntly illustrates its essential horror. More than any other character, Liu Tai-an embodies this truth. He is a terrifying figure who has lost all sense of human compassion and who torments his political rivals throughout the book. At a screening for the Chinese prisoners, Tai-an pressures the men to renounce Communism. Those who resist are beaten or killed. In the novel's most shocking scene, Tai-an first disembowels a man who resists his demands, and then eats the man's intestines. In contrast to the heroic language that surrounds war at the beginning of the novel, Liu Tai-an reflects its true nature.

Commissar Pei

The leader of Yu's military unit, Commissar Pei is a complex character whom Yu struggles to understand throughout the novel. At the beginning of the Korean War, Yu describes Pei as a respected leader whom the Chinese soldiers look up to. In contrast to others in the army, Pei values Yu for his intellect. He promotes Yu to the position of interpreter at the beginning of the war and comes to value his service greatly. For this reason, Yu feels close to Pei and strives not to let him down.

Yu views Commissar Pei as a man of honor, yet over the course of the novel his opinion of the leader begins to change. At Cheju Island, Yu approaches Pei after he learns that the Chinese prisoners plan an offensive against the Americans. The mission is suicidal, Yu warns, and he pleads with Pei to speak out against it. To his surprise, he learns that not only does Pei support the plan, but that he has ordered it. Pei admits that many Chinese will die, but he argues that the mission is worthwhile because it will bring international attention to the Chinese situation. The next day, the offensive goes forward and hundreds of Chinese are slaughtered. Yu holds Pei responsible and comes to see him in a new light. For Yu, Pei becomes a symbol of the tragic logic of war that values ideological principles over human life. Still, Yu remains loyal to Pei and supports the leader until the end of the novel.

General Bell

General Bell, the American commander in Compound 602 on Koje Island, is kidnapped by the Chinese in chapter 16. The Chinese believe that by capturing such a high-profile target they will draw international attention to their plight as prisoners of war. With General Bell in their custody, they organize a "Truth Commission" in which POWs testify to their abuse at the hands of the Americans. As part of the delegation that plots Bell's hearing, Yu gradually comes to a surprising understanding of the man. While at first he views him simply as a figurehead representing an unjust American POW policy, he eventually reaches a more sympathetic conclusion. Bell is shown to be a decent man who genuinely respects the Chinese. Despite his apparent position of power, he is simply following a policy dictated by his superiors. In this sense, his situation is similar to that of the Chinese soldiers.

Yu starts to see General Bell differently when he observes him one day talking on the phone with a fellow American. The man tells Bell that his wife is worried. "I went to see her just now," the man says. "She was crying, this is hard for her." In response, Bell tears up and asks the man to tell his wife that he is okay. Listening to their conversation, Yu is moved, realizing that Bell is a real person, not simply the "Enemy Leader" of Chinese propaganda. The next day at the Truth Commission, Bell apologizes for American abuses and signs an agreement to improve conditions for the POWs. This is considered a major victory for the Chinese, although Yu is saddened when he learns that General Bell has lost his position as a result of his capture. Ha Jin links General Bell to the Chinese POWs when he notes that Bell is punished for having "shamed" America. Like the Chinese, he has fought loyally for his country, only to be treated with contempt when he is captured.

Literary Reception of the Novel

War Trash was Ha Jin's first novel since *Waiting* and firmly established his international reputation. The book not only met but exceeded readers' and critics' hopes and high expectations. With this book, Ha Jin won the prestigious PEN/Faulkner Award for the second time, an honor only previously given to Philip Roth and John Edgar Wideman. *War Trash* was also a finalist for the Pulitzer Prize. The novel won Ha Jin a wider international audience and raised his profile in America.

Conclusion

"It wasn't supposed to work out this way," Ha Jin once told an interviewer, reflecting on the astonishing arc of his life. "This is not where I thought I'd be." When considering Ha Jin's remarkable writing career, it is worth remembering where he has come from. As a child he witnessed the horror of Mao's Cultural Revolution firsthand, forced to watch his mother taken from his family for long stretches at a time. And yet, growing up, his loyalty to China never wavered. Ha Jin persuaded his father to let him enter the People's Liberation Army while he was underage so that he could defend his country.

It wasn't until the Tiananmen Square massacre of 1989 that he could no longer reconcile his love for the Chinese people with a belief in his country's government. When he decided to leave his home country for America it was with the goal of honoring the lives of the Chinese people through his writing. "I knew I might fail. I wanted to write honestly about China and preserve its real history."

The stories and novels that followed this turning point in Ha Jin's life have examined the inner lives of the Chinese people, who suffer under an oppressive government, amid the horrors of war. Time and again, Ha Jin has shown how ideology masks people's shared desires: to live freely, express themselves fully, and find love and contentment. His writing powerfully demonstrates that life is precious and must be cherished, and that people of all races and beliefs have much in common. That Ha Jin has found a worldwide audience is a testament to the deeply universal quality of his writing. Although his work remains largely banned in China, his devoted audience continues to grow, anxious for the next piece of news Ha Jin has to share about the human experience.

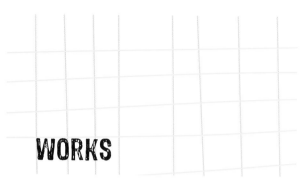

WORKS

Novels
In the Pond (1998)
Waiting (1999)
The Crazed (2002)
War Trash (2004)
A Free Life (2007)
Nanjing Requiem (2011)

Short Story Collections
Ocean of Words (1996)
Under the Red Flag (1997)
The Bridegroom (2000)
A Good Fall (2009)

Poetry
Between Silences (1990)
Facing Shadows (1996)
Wreckage (2001)

Nonfiction
The Writer as Migrant (2008)

Opera
The First Emperor – libretto co-written with Tan Dun *(2007)*

CHRONOLOGY

1956

February 21: Born Jin Xuefei in Jinzhou, China, to Jin Danlin and Zhao Yuafen.

1966

The Cultural Revolution begins. Ha Jin's mother is persecuted because her father was a former landlord and she is taken away to pick apples.

1970–1976

Ha Jin enrolls in the People's Liberation Army at thirteen, three years before the legal age. He is able to enter early because of his father's connections. He serves six years, first stationed on the Chinese-Soviet border and later trained as a telegraph operator.

1977

The Cultural Revolution ends and higher education is formally restored in China. Ha Jin becomes a member of first class to be admitted to a university, attending Heilongjiang University. He is assigned to study English, although it was his last choice for major.

1981

Graduates with a B.A. in English. He continues on for his M.A in English at Shandong University, completing his thesis on poet Robert Penn Warren.

Marries Lisha Bian.

1985

Ha Jin comes to the United States for his Ph.D. in English. He studies at Brandeis University, in Waltham, Massachusetts. He works as a busboy at a Chinese restaurant and a night watchman at a factory to support his wife and young son.

1989

Tiananmen Square massacre. More than one hundred protesters are killed for opposing the Chinese government. Ha Jin is horrified by this tragedy and decides he will not return to China. He commits to a writing career and soon after begins writing in English.

1990

Publishes first book of poetry, *Between Silences*.

1991

Begins M.F.A. in Creative Writing at Boston University.

1992

Earns his Ph.D. with a dissertation entitled, "The Universalization in Modern English and American Poetry: With Particular Reference to China."

1993

Becomes Assistant Professor in English at Emory University, in Atlanta, Georgia.

1996

Publishes first collection of stories, *Ocean of Words*. The book receives the Hemingway Foundation/PEN award for a first book of fiction by an American author. Ha Jin also publishes second book of poetry, *Facing Shadow*.

1997

Publishes the story collection, *Under the Red Flag*, which wins the Flannery O'Connor Award for Short Fiction.

1998

Publishes first novel, *In the Pond*.

1999

Receives Guggenheim Fellowship. His breakthrough novel, *Waiting*, is published. The novel wins the prestigious National Book Award and is a finalist for the Pulitzer Prize.

2000

Publishes the story collection, *The Bridegroom*. He wins PEN/Faulkner Award for *Waiting*.

2001

Publishes third book of poetry, *Wreckage*.

2002

Publishes *The Crazed*.

2004

War Trash is published and receives the PEN/Faulkner Award the following year.

2006

Gives a series of lectures at Rice University on the life of the migrant writer. These essays will later be published under the title, *The Writer as Migrant*, in 2008.

He collaborates with Tan Dun on libretto for the opera *The First Emperor*, which debuted at the Metropolitan Opera in New York.

2007

Publishes *A Free Life*.

2008

Receives Mary Ellen von der Heyden Fellowship in Fiction at the American Academy in Berlin, Germany. He publishes the essay collection, *The Writer as Migrant*.

2009

Publishes the story collection, *A Good Fall*.

2011

Publishes *Nanjing Requiem*.

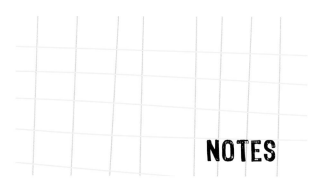

NOTES

All references to *Between Silences* are from *Between Silences*, University of Chicago Press, Chicago, 1990.

All references to *Ocean of Words* are from *Ocean of Words*, First Vintage International Edition, New York, 1998.

All references to *Under the Red Flag* are from *Under the Red Flag*, Zoland Books, Vermont, 1999.

All references to *In the Pond* are from *In the Pond*, First Vintage International, New York, 1998.

All references to *Waiting* are from *Waiting*, First Vintage International Edition, New York, 2000.

All references to *The Bridegroom* are from *The Bridegroom*, First Vintage International Edition, New York, 2000.

All references to *The Crazed* are from *The Crazed*, Pantheon-Random House, New York, 2002.

All references to *War Trash* are from *War Trash*, First Vintage International, New York, 2005.

All references to *The Migrant As Writer* are from *The Migrant as Writer*, University of Chicago Press, Chicago, 2006.

All references to *A Free Life* are from *A Free Life*, Pantheon-Random House, New York, 2007.

All references to *A Good Fall* are from *A Good Fall*, Pantheon-Random House, New York, 2009.

Introduction

p. 6, "speak for those . . . ": Ha Jin, *The Writer As Migrant*, Chicago: University of Chicago Press, 2006.

Chapter 1

p. 9, "I was glued . . . ": Greenberg, "Ha Jin Translates America," *Newsweek*, October 25, 2007.

p. 12, "All political power . . . ": "Chinese History: Mao Zedong," 2008, www.chinavoc.com/history/prc_sina/mzd.htm

p. 12, "My mother was . . . ": Garner, "Ha Jin's Cultural Revolution," *New York Times*, February 6, 2000.

p. 13, "There were millions . . . ": Greenberg, "Ha Jin Translates America," *Newsweek*, October 25, 2007.

p. 14, "I didn't like . . . ": Ha Jin, interview with the author, July 14, 2009.

p. 14, "Inside and outside . . . ": Weingberger, "Enormous Changes," *PEN America Interview Series*, 2005.

p. 15, "Like everyone else . . . ": Garner, "Ha Jin's Cultural Revolution," *New York Times*, February 6, 2000.

p. 18, "We were not . . . ": Ha Jin, Interview with the author, July 14, 2009.

p. 18, "Suddenly I felt . . . ": Weinberger, "Enormous Changes," *PEN America Interview Series*, 2005.

p. 18, "It was quite . . . ": Weinberger, "Enormous Changes," *PEN America Interview Series*, 2005.

p. 19, "I began to . . . ": Weinberger, "Enormous Changes," *PEN America Interview Series*, 2005.

p. 19, "I was still . . . ": Garner, "Ha Jin's Cultural Revolution," *New York Times*, February 6, 2000.

p. 21, "My first choice . . . ": Weinberger, "Enormous Changes," *PEN America Interview Series*, 2005.

p. 21, "That was humiliating . . . ": Weinberger, "Enormous Changes," *PEN America Interview Series*, 2005.

p. 21, "I simply couldn't . . . ": Garner, "Ha Jin's Cultural Revolution," *New York Times*, February 6, 2000.

p. 22, "The more people . . . ": Ha Jin, interview with the author, July 20, 2009.

p. 23, "Like everyone else . . . ": Garner, "Ha Jin's Cultural Revolution," *New York Times*, February 6, 2000.

p. 24, "This is a . . . ": interview with the author, July 20, 2009.

Chapter 2

p. 25, "My first years . . . ": Garner, "Ha Jin's Cultural Revolution," *New York Times*, February 6, 2000.

p. 25, "There is a . . . ": Garner, "Ha Jin's Cultural Revolution," *New York Times*, February 6, 2000.

p. 27, "Nature has been . . . ": Weinberger, "Enormous Changes," *PEN America Interview Series*, 2005.

p. 27, "There were so . . . ": Weinberger, "Enormous Changes," *PEN America Interview Series*, 2005.

p. 27, "I was just . . . ": Weinberger, "Enormous Changes," *PEN America Interview Series*, 2005.

p. 27, "It was extraordinary . . . ": Garner, "Ha Jin's Cultural Revolution," *New York Times*, February 6, 2000.

p. 31, "I was not . . . ": Garner, "Ha Jin's Cultural Revolution," *New York Times*, February 6, 2000.

p. 31, "I couldn't serve . . . ": Weinberger, "Enormous Changes," *PEN America Interview Series*, 2005.

p. 31, "In the chaos . . . ": Weinberger, "Enormous Changes," *PEN America Interview Series*, 2005.

p. 31, "When he landed . . . ": Weinberger, "Enormous Changes," *PEN America Interview Series*, 2005.

p. 32, "My wife encouraged me . . . ": Ha Jin, "Interview with Ha Jin," *The Paula Gordon Show*, November 8, 2000.

p. 32, "You don't write . . . ": Gordon, "Interview with Ha Jin," *The Paula Gordon Show*, November 8, 2000.

p. 33, "Speak for those . . . ": Ha Jin, *The Migrant as Writer*, Chicago, Chicago Press, 2006.

p. 33, "Not merely victims . . . ": Thomas, "Interview with Ha Jin," *Emory Magazine*, Spring 2008.

p. 34, "The real reason . . . ": Ha Jin, Interview with the Author, June 10, 2009.

p. 35, "I was driven . . . ": Weich, "Ha Jin Lets It Go," *Powells Bookstore Interview*, February 2, 2000.

p. 35, "For the initial . . . ": Gordon, "Interview with Ha Jin," *The Paula Gordon Show*, November 8, 2000.

Chapter 3

p. 40, "I was very . . . ": Ha Jin, Interview with the Author, May 23, 2009.

p. 41, "With history, we . . . ": Gordon, "Interview with Paula Gordon," *The Paula Gordon Show*, November 8, 2000.

p. 41, "Politics is only . . . ": Weich, "Ha Jin Lets It Go," *Powells Bookstore Interview*, February 2, 2000.

p. 45, "I want to . . . ": Ha Jin, Interview with the Author, May 23, 2009.

p. 48, "I have been . . . ": Ha Jin, *The Writer as Migrant*, 2008.

Chapter 4

p. 49, "After Waiting, I . . . ": Garner, "Ha Jin's Cultural Revolution," *New York Times*, Feb. 6, 2000.

p. 66, "Your banker would . . . ": Garner, "Ha Jin's Cultural Revolution," *New York Times*, Feb. 6, 2000.

p. 75, "Ha Jin has described . . . ": Weich, "Ha Jin Lets It Go," *Powells Bookstore Interview*, February 2, 2000.

p. 76, "Waiting provides a . . . ": *New York Times Book Review*, *Waiting* cover, 1999.

p. 76, "A simple love . . . ": Chicago Tribune, *Waiting* cover, 1999.

p. 77, "Maybe it's because . . . ": Gordon, "Interview with Ha Jin," *The Paula Gordon Show*, November 8, 2000.

Chapter 5

p. 97, "The best lack . . . ": Yeats, "The Second Coming," *Online Literature*.

p. 106, "It wasn't supposed . . . ": Garner, "Ha Jin's Cultural Revolution," *The New York Times*, February 6, 2000.

p. 106, "I knew I . . . ": Ha Jin, "Exiled to English," *New York Times*, May 30, 2009.

FURTHER INFORMATION

Books

Chen, Dad. *China's Son: Growing Up in the Cultural Revolution*. New York: Delacorte Press, 2001.

Moise, Edwin. *Modern China: A History Book*. Third Edition. New York: Longmen Press, 2008.

Simmie, Scott, and Bob Nixon. *Tiananmen Square*. Seattle: University of Washington Press, 1990.

Yu, Chun. *Little Green: Growing Up During the Chinese Cultural Revolution*. New York: Simon & Schuster, 2005.

Websites

Asian-American Literature and History

www.asian-nation.org/artists.shtml

Extensive resource for contemporary Asian-American writing, including discussion of themes in Ha Jin's work.

Ha Jin

www.georgiaencyclopedia.org/nge/Article.jsp?id=h-2843

Includes biographical information, discussion of key works, and suggested materials for further reading.

Interview with Ha Jin

www.nytimes.com/2004/10/10/books/review/1010books-garner.html

Excellent interview with Ha Jin on the writing of *War Trash*. Includes rare discussion of the political ideas that motivated the writing of this book.

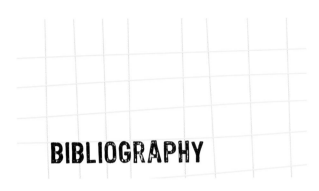

BIBLIOGRAPHY

Albanese, D. "A Word with the Writer." Interview with Ha Jin. *Collected Stories*, 2000, www.collectedstories.com/files/storyteller/hajin.html.

Burns, Caroleq. "Off the Page." Interview with Ha Jin. *Washington Post*, December 6, 2007, www.washingtonpost.com/wpdyn/content/discussion/2007/11/21/DI2007112101456.html.

Caswell, Michelle. "An Interview with Ha Jin." *Asia Source*, November 17, 2000, www.asiasource.org/arts/haHaJin.cfm .

Farnsworth, Elizabeth. "National Book Awards." Interview with Ha Jin. *PBS Online Newshour*, November 30, 1999, www.pbs.org/newshour/bb/entertainment/july-dec99/ha-HaJin_nba_11-30.html.

Garner, Dwight. "Somehow I Couldn't Stop." An Interview with Ha Jin. *New York Times*, October 10, 2004, www.nytimes.com/2004/10/10/books/review/101books-garner.html .

————. "Ha Jin's Cultural Revolution." *New York Times*, February 6, 2000, www.nytimes.com/2000/02/06/magazine/ha-HaJin-s-cultural-revolution.html.

Gogwilt, Chris. "An Interview with Ha Jin." *Guernica Magazine*, January 2007, www.guernicamag.com/interviews/258/post/.

Gordon, Paula. "Interview with Ha Jin." *The Paula Gordon Show*, November 8, 2000, www.paulagordon.com/shows/Ha Jin/ .

Greenberg, Susan H. "Ha Jin Translates America." *Newsweek*, October 25, 2007, www.newsweek.com/id/62103/page/1.

Ha Jin. "Exiled to English." *New York Times*, May 30, 2009, www.nytimes.com/2009/05/31/opinion/31haHa Jin.html.

Johnson, Sarah Anne. *The Very Telling: Conversations with American Writers.* Lebanon, NH: University Press of New England, 2006.

Li, Wenxin. "Ha Jin." In *Asian American Short Story Writers*, ed. Guiyou Huang. Westport: Greenwood Press, 2003.

Siciliano, Jana. "Author Profile: Ha Jin." Interview with Ha Jin. *Bookreporter*, October 13, 2000, www.bookreporter.com/authors/au-Ha Jin-ha.asp.

Thomas, John D. "Across an Ocean of Words." *Emory Magazine*, Spring 1998, www.emory.edu/EMORY_MAGAZINE/spring98/haHa Jin.html.

Weich, Dave. "Interview with Ha Jin." *Powells Books*, February 2000, www.terra-i.com/autoren/Ha Jin-interview.htm.

Weingberger, Eliot. "Enormous Changes." PEN America Interview Series, 2005, www.pen.org/viewmedia.php/prmMID/1416/prmID/1644.

Yeats, William Butler. "The Second Coming." Online Literature, www.online-literature.com/yeats/780.

Page numbers in **boldface** are illustrations and photographs.

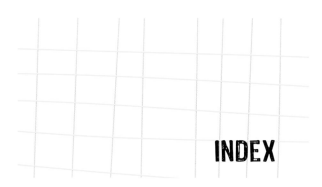

INDEX

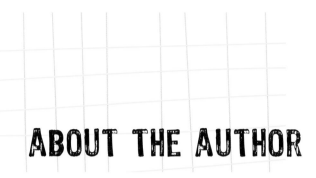

ABOUT THE AUTHOR

MARC SCHUMANN lives in Phoenix, Arizona, with his wife, Rebecca, and teaches English at Phoenix Community College. He completed his master's degree in English literature at Washington State University. *Ha Jin* is his first book for Cavendish Square.